MESSIANIC MENTALITY

GOD'S MASTER FORMULA FOR MASCULINE PURPOSE, POWER, AND PEACE

JOEL MAXWELL

ISBN: 979-8-218-78487-0

Printed in the USA

DEDICATION

To my fiancé, Sara, whom Adonai has sanctified for me,
To the faithful men who have walked before me—
Those who carried Torah scrolls and weathered storms,
Who built altars and raised godly seed,
Who proved that true strength kneels in prayer,
To the Prophets of old whom God used to preach His coming.
And to the One who makes broken men whole:
Yeshua, the Messiah, the ultimate example
Of surrendered strength.
Thank You for dying in our place for our sins,
We thank God for Your Resurrection,
And the Ruach HaKodesh for revealing this truth to us.

TABLE OF CONTENTS

PREFACE

Brothers,

This book was born from my own failures. I've been the man who confused dominance with leadership, who buried sadness under busyness, who thought provision was merely a paycheck. But through Scripture's lens—and the relentless grace of Yeshua—I discovered that God's design for masculinity is neither passive nor predatory. It is power under covenant.

Within these pages, you'll find no pop psychology or empty platitudes. Only the unchanging truth: You were made to reflect the Divine. Whether you're wrestling with pride, grief, or the weight of responsibility, Messianic Mentality will equip you to redeem every emotion and role according to God's will.

The world needs men forged in Messiah's image. Let this book be your anvil.

—Joel Maxwell

INTRODUCTION: THE CALL TO AUTHENTIC MASCULINITY

This book is not written to comfort the comfortable or affirm the status quo. Neither is it intended as mere intellectual exercise to be consumed and forgotten. Rather, it stands as both mirror and blueprint—exposing the spiritual poverty of contemporary masculinity while illuminating the ancient paths of godly manhood established by the Almighty Himself. The pages that follow demand more than casual reading; they require sincere teshuvah—a genuine turning of heart and mind toward the Creator's original design for men.

The divine purpose embedded within these chapters is to awaken men of every generation to their sacred calling, to convict hearts grown cold toward spiritual responsibility, and to ignite within each reader an unquenchable desire to become what Scripture defines as a man after God's own heart. In our present age, where authentic biblical masculinity has become as rare as a needle in a haystack, this work serves as both clarion call and practical guide for those willing to abandon cultural counterfeits in pursuit of divine authenticity.

As the Psalmist declares, *"How blessed is the man who does not walk in the counsel of the wicked, nor stand in the path of sinners, nor sit in the seat of scoffers! But his delight is in the Torah of Adonai, and on His Torah he meditates day and night" (Psalm 1:1-2, TLV).* The man described here stands in stark contrast to the emasculated specimens produced by our contemporary culture—men who have traded their spiritual birthright for the pottage of immediate gratification and cultural acceptance.

The Systematic Destruction of Biblical Manhood

The current crisis of masculinity represents more than mere societal decay; it constitutes a deliberate, systematic assault on the divine order established at creation. When the Almighty formed Adam from the dust of the earth and breathed into his nostrils the breath of life, He established not merely a biological entity, but a spiritual being created in the image of God *(Genesis 1:27, TLV)* with distinct roles, responsibilities, and divine expectations.

Yet observe the contemporary landscape: men have been systematically stripped of their God-ordained roles through decades of cultural manipulation and spiritual warfare. The enemy of our souls, understanding that as goes the man, so goes the family, and as goes the family, so goes the nation, has orchestrated a multi-pronged attack on masculine identity, purpose, and spiritual authority.

The assault begins in childhood, where toxic media programming infiltrates young minds through screens that babysit more than parents guide. Children consume thousands of hours of content that portrays men as bumbling fools, sexual predators, or unnecessary appendages to family life. The entertainment industrial complex—controlled by forces hostile to biblical truth—systematically programs the next generation to view traditional masculinity as toxic while promoting gender confusion and moral relativism.

Simultaneously, political operatives have waged war on the spiritual foundations of society, methodically removing the knowledge of God from schools, courthouses, and increasingly, from churches themselves. The result is generations of men raised without the moral compass provided by divine revelation, left to navigate life's complexities with nothing but their fallen nature as guide.

The Intellectual and Spiritual Bankruptcy of Modern Men

The Prophet Hosea's ancient lament rings with prophetic accuracy in our generation: My people are destroyed for lack of knowledge. Because you have rejected knowledge, I also will reject you from being priest for Me; because you have forgotten the Torah of your God, I will also forget your children *(Hosea 4:6, TLV)*. This divine indictment perfectly describes the contemporary crisis of masculinity.

Modern men, severed from the wellspring of divine wisdom found in Scripture, have become intellectually anemic and spiritually impotent. They lack the fundamental knowledge of spiritual realities that would enable them to discern truth from deception, righteousness from wickedness, and their divine calling from cultural programming. Without the transforming power of God's Word actively working in their hearts and minds, they remain slaves to their base impulses—sexually promiscuous, emotionally unstable, and morally compromised.

This spiritual ignorance manifests in practical ways: men who cannot control their sexual appetites, who lack the self-discipline to delay gratification, who abandon their responsibilities when circumstances become difficult, and who seek meaning in material possessions rather than eternal purposes. They have become, in the words of the Apostle Paul, *lovers of themselves, lovers of money, boastful, proud, abusive, disobedient to their parents, ungrateful, unholy, without love, unforgiving, slanderous, without self-control, brutal, not lovers of the good, treacherous, rash, conceited, lovers of pleasure rather than lovers of God (2 Timothy 3:2-4, TLV)*.

The root cause remains consistent: these men have never been properly taught how to study and apply the Word of God. They remain ignorant of spiritual principles that would govern their thoughts, emotions, and actions. Without divine illumination, they stumble through life making decisions based on immediate gratification rather than eternal consequences.

The Devastating Consequences of Absent Fathers

The statistical evidence reveals the catastrophic results of men abandoning their God-ordained roles. Over 18 million children in

America grow up without fathers in their homes—a staggering 25% of all children in the nation. This represents not merely a sociological phenomenon but a spiritual crisis of unprecedented proportions.

Scripture establishes the father as the primary spiritual leader of the household, responsible for teaching God's commands to his children: *These words, which I am commanding you today, shall be on your heart. You are to teach them diligently to your children, and speak of them when you sit in your house, when you walk by the way, when you lie down and when you rise up (Deuteronomy 6:6-7, TLV).*

When fathers abandon this sacred trust—whether through physical absence, emotional detachment, or spiritual passivity—the consequences reverberate through generations. Children grow up without proper models of godly masculinity, daughters develop distorted expectations of men, and sons lack the guidance necessary to become men of integrity themselves.

The enemy has successfully weaponized entertainment culture to normalize and even glorify paternal irresponsibility. Music lyrics celebrate baby daddies over committed husbands, television programs mock traditional family structures, and social media influences promote sexual promiscuity over covenant commitment. Young men, lacking proper spiritual instruction, embrace these destructive patterns as normal expressions of masculinity.

The Spiritual Warfare Behind Cultural Decay

The Apostle Paul warned that *our struggle is not against flesh and blood, but against the rulers, against the authorities, against the cosmic powers over this present darkness, against the spiritual forces of evil in the heavenly places (Ephesians 6:12, TLV).* The current crisis of masculinity must be understood within this framework of spiritual warfare.

The enemy's strategy targets the fundamental building block of society: the family unit established by God at creation. By corrupting men—the designated spiritual leaders of their households—Satan effectively neutralizes entire family lines and removes godly influence from future generations.

This warfare manifests through multiple vectors: pornography addictions that destroy men's ability to love their wives sacrificially; material obsessions that redirect their focus from eternal to temporal concerns; entertainment addictions that consume time meant for spiritual growth and family leadership; and philosophical deceptions that convince them their roles as husbands and fathers are outdated social constructs rather than divine callings.

The tragic irony is that many men caught in these destructive patterns still claim to believe in God or follow Yeshua, yet their lives demonstrate complete ignorance of what genuine discipleship requires. They have embraced a shallow, culturally accommodated version of faith that demands nothing and transforms nothing.

The Path Forward: Seven Pillars of Biblical Masculinity

The solution to this crisis lies not in cultural programs or psychological theories, but in returning to the eternal principles established by the Creator Himself. The chapters that follow will systematically examine seven foundational aspects of biblical masculinity, each supported by thorough scriptural exposition and practical application.

Chapter I: A Man of God establishes the foundational relationship that must govern all other aspects of masculine identity. Before a man can properly fulfill any earthly role, he must first understand his position before the Almighty, his dependence upon divine grace, and his calling to live as a covenant keeper in a covenant-breaking world. This chapter examines what it means to walk with God as Enoch walked, to find favor like Noah, and to demonstrate the faith of Abraham.

Chapter II: A Provider explores the divine mandate given to Adam to work and keep the Garden, examining how this calling extends to every man's responsibility to provide for his household through honest labor, wise stewardship, and trust in God's provision. Far from mere materialism, this role encompasses physical, emotional, and spiritual provision that creates security and stability for those under his care.

Chapter III: A Protector delves into the masculine calling to stand guard over those entrusted to his care, following the example of Nehemiah rebuilding Jerusalem's walls. This protection encompasses physical safety, emotional security, and spiritual covering, requiring both strength and wisdom to discern genuine threats from false alarms.

Chapter IV: A Leader examines servant leadership as demonstrated by Moses, Joshua, and ultimately by Messiah Himself. True biblical leadership serves rather than dominates, guides rather than controls, and takes responsibility rather than shifting blame. This chapter distinguishes authentic spiritual authority from worldly power structures.

Chapter V: A Husband explores the sacred covenant of marriage as established by God and exemplified in Messiah's relationship with His bride, the believing community. This chapter examines the husband's role as loving head of his household, called to sacrifice himself for his wife's sanctification and growth.

Chapter VI: A Father investigates the paternal calling to raise children in the discipline and instruction of the Lord *(Ephesians 6:4, TLV)*, following the examples of godly fathers throughout Scripture who prioritized their children's spiritual development over material success or social acceptance.

Chapter VII: A Builder concludes with the comprehensive vision of men as builders of lasting legacies—spiritual, familial, and cultural institutions that honor God and serve future generations. Like

Nehemiah reconstructing Jerusalem or Solomon building the Temple, godly men are called to create rather than merely consume.

Each chapter approaches these roles from three integrated perspectives: Spiritual Application (how these principles function in the realm of spiritual warfare and divine relationship), Emotional Application (how biblical masculinity properly channels and directs emotional responses), and Physical Application (how these principles manifest in practical, observable behaviors and decisions).

The Urgent Need for Spiritual Awakening

The hour is late, and the need is urgent. Every day that passes without genuine spiritual awakening among men results in more fatherless children, more broken marriages, more confused youth, and more communities stripped of godly influence. The enemy's assault on biblical masculinity accelerates with each passing year, becoming more sophisticated and more successful in its destructive goals.

Yet hope remains. The same God who called Abraham from Ur, who raised up Moses to deliver Israel, who transformed Saul into Paul, continues to call men to abandon cultural conformity and embrace their divine destiny. Throughout history, spiritual renewals have begun when individual men chose to reject the spirit of their age and align themselves completely with God's revealed will.

The five emotions that govern human experience—love, fear, anger, sadness, and envy—will be examined through the lens of Scripture to provide practical tools for emotional maturity and spiritual growth. Understanding how to properly channel these God-given emotions according to biblical principles represents a crucial aspect of masculine development too often ignored in contemporary discipleship.

This work ultimately depends not upon human effort alone but upon the transforming power of the Ruach HaKodesh (Holy Spirit) working through surrendered hearts. As the Prophet Zechariah declared, *"Not by might nor by power, but by My Ruach, says Adonai-Tzva'ot (Zechariah 4:6, TLV).* Yet divine power flows through human vessels willing to align themselves completely with divine purposes.

The prayer accompanying this work is that the Almighty would use these words to raise up a generation of men who refuse to accept cultural substitutes for biblical authenticity—men who will pay any price to fulfill their God-ordained roles as spiritual leaders, faithful husbands, devoted fathers, and builders of righteousness in an unrighteous generation.

The call has been sounded. The choice remains: Will this generation of men answer the call to authentic biblical masculinity, or will they continue sleepwalking through lives of spiritual mediocrity while their families, communities, and culture collapse around them?

The time for comfortable compromise has ended. The hour for radical obedience has arrived.

CHAPTER ONE: THE DIVINE CALLING OF A MAN OF GOD

The Deception of Self-Assessment

In the recesses of every man's heart echoes a question that reverberates through the corridors of eternity: "Am I truly a Man of God?" When confronted with this inquiry, the vast majority of men respond with unhesitating confidence, "Yes, of course." Yet beneath this confident veneer lies a profound misunderstanding of what it means to bear such a sacred designation. The tragedy of our generation is not that men fail to claim this title, but that they claim it with such casual presumption, devoid of any comprehension of the weighty divine expectations that accompany this holy calling.

Contemporary society has systematically reduced the concept of a Man of God to a mere caricature—a Sunday morning performance of religious theatrics, a collection of spiritual clichés, and a veneer of piety that crumbles under the relentless scrutiny of daily living. The world celebrates the man who occupies a pew regularly, contributes financially to religious institutions, and punctuates his speech with "hallelujah," "amen," and "praise the Lord." Women, tragically influenced by this shallow interpretation, seek husbands who exhibit these superficial markers, mistaking religious activity for spiritual authenticity. This massive deception has spawned a generation of men who wear the title "Man of God" like an ill-fitting garment, never comprehending the transformative power it should represent in their lives.

The Hebrew Scriptures present a stark contrast to this modern misrepresentation. The term ish Elohim (man of God) appears throughout the Tanakh as a designation of extraordinary honor, reserved exclusively for those who had surrendered their lives completely to HaShem's purposes. These were men like Moshe, who spoke with the Almighty face to face; Eliyahu, who called down fire from heaven; and David, who was described as "a man after God's own heart." They were not merely religious practitioners but vessels of divine power, instruments of heavenly purpose, and reflections of God's character in a fallen world.

The Two Assemblies: Visible and Invisible

The Scriptures reveal a profound truth that pierces to the very heart of authentic faith: the existence of two distinct assemblies that share the same designation yet possess vastly different natures. The Hebrew word Kehillah refers to a gathering or assembly of people, while the Greek Ekklesia means "a calling out"—those who are called out from the world system. This divine calling creates two distinct groups operating under the same spiritual terminology but possessing fundamentally different spiritual realities.

The visible assembly encompasses those who gather in physical locations, participating in religious activities and identifying themselves as believers. However, as Yeshua warned His talmidim (disciples), even within these sacred spaces, spiritual wolves prowl among the sheep:

Mattityahu 7:15-16, TLV

"Beware of false prophets, who come to you in sheep's clothing, but inwardly they are ravenous wolves. You will know them by their fruits. Do men gather grapes from thornbushes or figs from thistles?"

This warning transcends its immediate historical context, speaking prophetically to every generation about the reality of spiritual deception within religious institutions. The false prophets Messiah described represent not merely external enemies but internal threats—those who claim divine authority while serving satanic purposes. These individuals manipulate Scripture to justify ungodly

11

agendas, creating doctrines that appear spiritual but lead to destruction.

The parable of the wheat and tares further illuminates this sobering reality:

Mattityahu13:24-26, TLV

"The kingdom of heaven may be compared to a man who sowed good seed in his field. But while men slept, his enemy came and sowed weeds among the wheat and went his way. But when the grain sprouted and produced a crop, then the weeds appeared also."

When the servants discovered the weeds, they asked whether they should remove them immediately. The master's response reveals divine wisdom:

Mattityahu 13:29-30, TLV

"No, lest while you gather up the weeds you also uproot the wheat with them. Let both grow together until the harvest, and at the time of harvest I will say to the reapers, 'First gather together the weeds and bind them in bundles to burn them, but gather the wheat into my barn.'"

Messiah's interpretation of this parable exposes the startling truth:

Mattityahu 13:37-39, TLV

"The one who sows the good seed is the Son of Man; the field is the world. As for the good seed, these are the people who belong to the Kingdom; and the weeds are the people who belong to the Evil One. The enemy who sows them is the Adversary, the harvest is the end of the age, and the harvesters are angels."

The implications are staggering: within the visible assembly, genuine believers (wheat) coexist with counterfeit professors (tares) until the final harvest. Not everyone who claims faith possesses it, not everyone who speaks of God truly knows Him, and not everyone who performs religious activities has experienced authentic spiritual transformation.

In stark contrast, the invisible assembly consists exclusively of genuine believers—those who have encountered the living God and experienced authentic spiritual transformation through the resurrection power of Yeshua HaMashiach. These are the ones who have been "born again" (born from above), sealed by the Ruach HaKodesh (Holy Spirit), and possess a conscience made pure through the blood of the Lamb. A true Man of God emerges from this invisible, spiritual assembly, distinguished not by external religious performance but by internal spiritual reality.

The Spiritual Battlefield: Learning to See Beyond the Veil

The greatest hindrance confronting modern men in their spiritual development is their inability to perceive spiritual realities. We have been systematically conditioned to trust exclusively in our five physical senses—sight, hearing, touch, taste, and smell—while remaining completely blind to the spiritual realm where the authentic battle for souls rages unceasingly. This sensory imprisonment leaves us vulnerable to satanic deception and spiritual attack.

The Apostle Kefa (Peter) delivered a sobering warning about this very danger:

1 Kefa 5:8-9, TLV

"Stay sober, stay alert! Your enemy the devil prowls around like a roaring lion, seeking someone to devour. Resist him, firm in your faith, knowing that the same kinds of suffering are being experienced by your brotherhood throughout the world."

This warning carried particular significance for Jewish believers who were transitioning from a legalistic understanding of Torah observance to a faith-based relationship with Messiah. The concept of spiritual vigilance was foreign to those accustomed to external religious observance and ritual performance. Yet Yeshua Himself operated constantly through spiritual perception, possessing the fullness of the Ruach and demonstrating perfect discernment in every situation.

The Apostle Paul illuminated this spiritual reality:

Ephesians 6:12, TLV
"For our struggle is not against flesh and blood, but against the rulers, against the powers, against the world forces of this darkness, against the spiritual forces of wickedness in the heavenly places."

The Greek word translated "struggle" (pale) refers to hand-to-hand combat, wrestling, and intense physical conflict. This reveals that spiritual warfare is not theoretical but intensely practical, affecting every aspect of daily life. The "rulers" (archas) and "powers" (exousias) represent organized demonic hierarchies with specific assignments and territorial authority.

Consider the dramatic difference between spiritual and carnal responses to identical circumstances:

The Carnal Response: A close friend approaches you with seemingly innocent conversation, gradually steering the discussion toward inappropriate topics. He comments on the physical attributes of a married woman walking nearby, making suggestive remarks about her appearance. Operating solely through physical senses, you remain completely unaware of the spiritual manipulation occurring. You engage in lustful thoughts, participate in inappropriate conversation, and sin against both God and the woman's husband. The enemy has successfully led you into compromise, providing legal grounds for accusation and reducing your spiritual effectiveness.

The Spiritual Response: The identical scenario unfolds, but you operate through spiritual discernment provided by the Holy Spirit. You recognize the subtle shift in conversation as a deliberate satanic strategy designed to ensnare you. Your spirit bears witness to the inappropriate nature of the discussion. You respond with wisdom, either redirecting the conversation toward edifying topics or boldly addressing the sin. You maintain your spiritual integrity while potentially ministering to your friend's spiritual need.

The fundamental difference between these responses lies not in the external circumstances but in the spiritual lens through which they are perceived and processed. The Man of God must develop the supernatural ability to see beyond the physical realm into the spiritual dynamics that govern all human interaction.

The Messiah's Model: Victory Through the Word

The wilderness temptation of Yeshua provides the perfect template for understanding and conducting spiritual warfare. After forty days of fasting, weakened physically but strengthened spiritually, Messiah faced the Adversary's most strategic and sophisticated attacks. Each temptation was precisely designed to prevent His redemptive mission, yet each was overcome through the strategic and accurate application of Scripture.

Luke 4:1-2, TLV

"Then Yeshua, filled with the Ruach HaKodesh, returned from the Jordan and was led by the Spirit in the wilderness for forty days, being tempted by the devil. And He ate nothing during those days, and when they were ended, He was hungry."

Note the critical detail that must not be overlooked: Yeshua was "led by the Spirit" into this season of testing. This reveals that God Himself orchestrates situations that examine our spiritual maturity and character. The Greek word "temptation" (peirasmos) fundamentally means "testing" or "trial"—not an evil enticement but a divine examination of spiritual authenticity. Just as gold is refined through intense fire, our faith is purified and strengthened through divinely permitted testing.

When the Adversary challenged Yeshua to transform stones into bread, directly addressing His physical hunger and human needs, Messiah responded with precision from *Deuteronomy 8:3*:

Luke 4:4, TLV

"But He answered and said, 'It is written, "Man shall not live by bread alone, but by every word that proceeds from the mouth of God.""'

This response revealed that physical sustenance, while necessary, is secondary to spiritual nourishment. The Man of God understands that his ultimate survival depends not on material provision but on intimate relationship with the Living Word of God.

The second temptation offered all the kingdoms of the world and their glory in exchange for worship. This was not merely about acquiring temporal power but about methodology and timing. The Adversary offered a shortcut to Messiah's destined rulership, bypassing the cross and its redemptive necessity. Again, Yeshua responded with unerring precision from Scripture:

Luke 4:8, TLV

"And Yeshua answered and said to him, 'Get behind Me, Satan! For it is written, "You shall worship Adonai your God, and Him only you shall serve.""'

The third temptation demonstrated the Adversary's cunning sophistication, as Satan himself quoted Scripture, encouraging Yeshua to leap from the temple pinnacle. This misuse of God's Word demonstrates the enemy's ability to twist Scripture for destructive purposes—a tactic consistently employed by false teachers throughout history. Yet Messiah responded with perfect understanding:

Luke 4:12, TLV

"And Yeshua answered and said to him, 'It has been said, "You shall not put Adonai your God to the test.""'

Each response originated from the Torah, specifically from the book of Deuteronomy. This was not random Scripture quotation but strategic spiritual warfare conducted through precise application of divine truth. Yeshua demonstrated that victory over temptation emerges through deep, personal knowledge of God's Word combined with the supernatural power of the Holy Spirit.

The Man of God must follow this exact pattern, developing such intimate familiarity with Scripture that appropriate verses emerge spontaneously during moments of testing. This requires consistent, systematic study, meditative reflection, and practical application of biblical truth until it becomes the automatic response to every spiritual challenge.

The Discipline of Divine Awareness

Authentic spiritual maturity manifests through constant awareness of God's presence and activity in every circumstance. The Man of God trains himself to recognize the divine hand in every situation, from the most mundane daily occurrence to the most dramatic life-altering event. This awareness transforms every moment into an opportunity for worship and every challenge into an avenue for spiritual growth and divine glory.

The prophet Yesha'yahu (Isaiah) experienced this profound divine awareness during his commissioning:

Yesha'yahu 6:1-3, TLV

"In the year that King Uzziah died, I saw the Lord sitting on a throne, high and lifted up, and the train of His robe filled the temple. Above it stood seraphim; each one had six wings: with two he covered his face, with two he covered his feet, and with two he flew. And one cried to another and said: 'Holy, holy, holy is Adonai-Tzva'ot; the whole earth is full of His glory!'"

The seraphim's continuous worship demonstrates the appropriate response to divine holiness. Their cry of "Holy, holy, holy" represents not mere repetition but escalating recognition of God's infinite purity, majesty, and transcendence. These angelic beings, who dwell constantly in God's presence, never cease their worship because they continuously discover new dimensions of divine glory.

This same God who spoke the universe into existence, who numbers every star and calls them by name, who holds the breath of every living creature in His hands, deserves constant acknowledgment and praise. Yet how frequently do we actually recognize His presence in our daily lives? How often do we acknowledge His provision in our very breath, our heartbeat, our ability to see and hear and move? The Man of God develops a heart of gratitude that responds to divine goodness with immediate praise, whether expressed audibly or cherished in the secret chambers of the heart.

The Symphony of Praise: Recognizing God's Grace in All Things

The Psalmist captured the essence of comprehensive, continuous praise in the final psalm of the Psalter:

Tehillim 150:1-6, TLV

"Praise Adonai! Praise God in His sanctuary; praise Him in His mighty expanse! Praise Him for His mighty acts; praise Him according to His excellent greatness! Praise Him with the sound of the shofar; praise Him with the harp and lyre! Praise Him with tambourine and dancing; praise Him with stringed instruments and flute! Praise Him with loud cymbals; praise Him with resounding cymbals! Let everything that has breath praise Adonai. Hallelujah!"

This magnificent psalm reveals that praise should be comprehensive, encompassing every aspect of existence and utilizing every available means of expression. The Man of God recognizes that every breath is a divine gift, every heartbeat a supernatural miracle, every day a sacred blessing from the hand of the Almighty. He understands that praise is not confined to moments of prosperity and success but extends through every season of life, including times of difficulty, testing, and apparent defeat.

The Hebrew word hallelujah literally means "Praise Yah" (the shortened form of YHVH), and it appears as both the opening and closing declaration of this psalm. This bracketing demonstrates that praise should frame every aspect of life—beginning each day with acknowledgment of God's goodness and concluding each evening with gratitude for His faithfulness.

Consider the infinite opportunities for praise that present themselves throughout a single day:

Morning Mercies: The gift of awakening from sleep, the restoration of consciousness, the provision of breath and strength, the opportunity to serve God in a new day. As the prophet Yirmeyahu (Jeremiah) declared: *"It is of Adonai's loving-kindnesses that we are not consumed, because His compassions do not fail. They are new every morning; great is Your faithfulness"* **(Eichah 3:22-23, TLV).**

Daily Provisions: Food for nourishment, water for hydration, shelter for protection, clothing for covering, employment for financial provision. Each represents God's covenant faithfulness to provide for His people's needs according to His promise: *"Therefore do not worry, saying, 'What shall we eat?' or 'What shall we drink?' or 'What shall we wear?' For the Gentiles seek after all these things, and your heavenly Father knows that you need all these things"* **(Mattityahu 6:31-32, TLV).**

Relational Blessings: Family members who share the journey, friends who provide fellowship and encouragement, opportunities to minister to others' needs, the incredible privilege of prayer and worship. The Man of God recognizes that relationships are divine gifts designed to reflect God's love and character.

Spiritual Realities: Salvation through Messiah's atoning sacrifice, the indwelling presence of the Holy Spirit, direct access to the Father through prayer, the promise of eternal life, the hope of resurrection. These spiritual blessings far exceed any material provision and warrant continuous gratitude.

Physical Capabilities: The ability to walk, run, work, see, hear, touch, taste, and smell—each sense functioning as a window into God's creative majesty. The intricate design of the human body testifies to divine wisdom and craftsmanship.

Protection and Guidance: Divine preservation from seen and unseen dangers, wisdom for decision-making, peace in uncertainty, strength for challenges. The Man of God acknowledges that *"the angel of Adonai encamps around those who fear Him, and rescues them" (Tehillim 34:7, TLV)*.

The Man of God trains his heart to recognize these blessings automatically, responding with gratitude and praise throughout each day. This practice transforms ordinary moments into worship experiences and maintains spiritual focus amid life's inevitable distractions and challenges.

Praise in the Darkness: The Test of Authentic Faith

Perhaps the most profound expression of spiritual maturity occurs when the Man of God maintains his posture of praise during seasons of difficulty, disappointment, and apparent defeat. This represents the ultimate test of faith—not praising God because of favorable circumstances, but praising Him despite unfavorable circumstances.

The prophet Chavakuk (Habakkuk) demonstrated this principle magnificently:

Chavakuk 3:17-19, TLV

"Though the fig tree does not bud and there are no grapes on the vines, though the olive crop fails and the fields produce no food, though there are no sheep in the pen and no cattle in the stalls, yet I will rejoice in Adonai, I will be joyful in God my Savior. Adonai Elohim is my strength; He makes my feet like the feet of a deer, He enables me to tread on the heights."

This declaration represents radical faith—praising God not for what He provides but for who He is. The prophet envisioned complete economic collapse, agricultural failure, and material devastation, yet his response was worship rather than worry, praise rather than panic. He understood that God's character remains unchanged regardless of circumstances, and His promises remain valid regardless of present appearances.

The Man of God embraces this same perspective, recognizing that praise during difficulty demonstrates genuine faith while praise during prosperity may simply reflect gratitude for blessing. When Job lost his wealth, his children, and his health, his initial response was worship:

Iyov 1:21, TLV

"Naked I came from my mother's womb, and naked I will return. Adonai gave and Adonai has taken away; blessed be the name of Adonai."

This response reveals spiritual maturity that transcends circumstances. Job understood that everything he possessed was a gift from God, held in stewardship rather than ownership. His praise reflected recognition of God's sovereignty rather than denial of present pain.

The Man of God develops this same spiritual perspective, understanding that difficult circumstances often serve divine purposes. They may be designed to develop character, strengthen faith, redirect priorities, or prepare for greater service. Rather than demanding explanations for suffering, he maintains confidence in God's wisdom and goodness.

The Characteristics of a Man of God

The Scriptures delineate specific characteristics that distinguish a genuine Man of God from mere religious practitioners. These traits represent not human achievements but divine transformations produced through intimate relationship with the Living God.

Uncompromising Devotion to the God of Israel

The Man of God demonstrates absolute loyalty to the God of Abraham, Isaac, and Jacob—the God who revealed Himself through Moses, spoke through the prophets, and became incarnate in Yeshua HaMashiach. This devotion supersedes all other loyalties and commitments.

Devarim 6:4-5, TLV

"Hear, O Israel: Adonai our God, Adonai is one! You shall love Adonai your God with all your heart, with all your soul, and with all your strength."

The Hebrew word translated "love" (ahav) encompasses not merely emotion but complete commitment, loyalty, and dedication. This love affects every aspect of life—thoughts, emotions, decisions, relationships, and priorities. The Man of God arranges his entire existence around this central commitment to God.

This devotion manifests through various practical expressions:

Priority in Time: The Man of God prioritizes time with God through prayer, Scripture study, and worship. He understands that this relationship requires consistent nurturing and attention.

Priority in Resources: He demonstrates his devotion through generous giving to God's work, supporting those in need, and using his material resources to advance God's kingdom.

Priority in Relationships: While loving family and friends deeply, he maintains God as his ultimate loyalty. When human relationships conflict with divine commands, he chooses obedience to God.

Priority in Decisions: Every major decision is submitted to God for wisdom and direction. The Man of God seeks divine guidance rather than relying solely on human wisdom or popular opinion.

Unwavering Commitment to Biblical Truth

The Man of God anchors his beliefs, values, and practices in the unchanging truth of Scripture. He recognizes that God's Word provides the ultimate authority for faith and practice, transcending cultural trends and popular opinions.

Tehillim 119:105, TLV
"Your word is a lamp to my feet and a light to my path."

This verse reveals Scripture's practical function in daily life. The Hebrew word for "lamp" (ner) refers to a small oil lamp that provides immediate illumination for the next step, while "light" (or) suggests broader illumination for the overall direction. The Man of God uses Scripture for both immediate decisions and long-term planning.

This commitment to biblical truth requires:

Consistent Study: The Man of God maintains regular, systematic study of Scripture, seeking to understand God's will and ways. He approaches the Bible not as a collection of inspirational thoughts but as divine revelation requiring careful interpretation and application.

Accurate Interpretation: He interprets Scripture through proper hermeneutical principles, considering historical context, original language meanings, and consistent theological framework. He avoids eisegesis (reading into the text) while practicing exegesis (drawing meaning from the text).

Practical Application: Biblical knowledge must translate into practical living. The Man of God applies scriptural principles to his relationships, work, finances, and personal conduct.

Defensive Apologetics: He is prepared to defend biblical truth against false teaching and secular attack. This requires understanding both Scripture and the contemporary challenges to faith.

Moral Purity and Integrity

The Man of God maintains high moral standards, understanding that personal holiness reflects God's character and validates his spiritual authority. This purity extends to all areas of life—thought, word, and deed.

Tehillim 24:3-4, TLV

"Who may ascend into the hill of Adonai? Who may stand in His holy place? He who has clean hands and a pure heart, who has not lifted up his soul to an idol, nor sworn deceitfully."

The "clean hands" represent righteous actions, while the "pure heart" indicates right motivations. The Man of God understands that external behavior must flow from internal transformation. He avoids not only sinful actions but sinful attitudes and motivations.

This moral purity manifests in several specific areas:

Sexual Purity: The Man of God maintains strict sexual purity, reserving intimate physical expression for marriage. He guards his eyes, his thoughts, and his associations to protect this area of life. This does not mean that a renewed man in the Messiah cannot be pure again. Therefore, what this means is that the man of God is to maneuver as if he were pure as he pursues righteousness, waiting until marriage.

Financial Integrity: He conducts all financial dealings with complete honesty, treating employees, customers, and business partners with fairness and respect. He avoids deceptive practices even when they might provide advantage.

Truthfulness: The Man of God is known for his truthfulness, avoiding lies, exaggerations, and deceptive statements. His word can be trusted completely.

Humility: He demonstrates genuine humility, recognizing his dependence on God's grace and avoiding pride or arrogance. He readily admits mistakes and seeks forgiveness when necessary.

Sacrificial Love and Service

The Man of God follows Messiah's example of sacrificial love, seeking others' welfare above his own comfort and convenience. This love extends beyond mere sentiment to practical action and personal sacrifice.

1 Yochanan 3:16, TLV

"By this we know love, because He laid down His life for us. And we also ought to lay down our lives for the brethren."

This verse reveals that authentic love is defined by sacrifice rather than sentiment. The Man of God demonstrates this love through various expressions:

Sacrificial Marriage: He loves his wife as Messiah loved the church, seeking her spiritual, emotional, and physical welfare above his own preferences and desires.

Devoted Fatherhood: He invests time, energy, and resources in his children's spiritual development, education, and character formation. He prioritizes their needs over his personal recreation and comfort.

Generous Friendship: He demonstrates loyalty, support, and encouragement to friends, even when such support requires personal sacrifice or inconvenience.

Community Service: He seeks opportunities to serve others in his community, understanding that practical service validates verbal testimony about God's love.

Spiritual Discernment and Wisdom

The Man of God develops supernatural discernment that enables him to distinguish between truth and error, good and evil, divine and demonic influences. This discernment protects him from deception while enabling him to guide others effectively.

Hebrews 5:14, TLV

"But solid food belongs to those who are of full age, that is, those who by reason of use have their senses exercised to discern both good and evil."

This verse reveals that spiritual discernment develops through maturity and practice. The Man of God sharpens his spiritual senses through consistent exposure to Scripture, prayer, and the guidance of the Holy Spirit.

This discernment manifests in various ways:

Doctrinal Discernment: He can identify false teaching and unbiblical practices, protecting himself and others from spiritual deception.

Relational Discernment: He recognizes the spiritual condition and motivations of others, enabling him to minister appropriately and avoid harmful relationships.

Situational Discernment: He perceives the spiritual dynamics operating in various situations, enabling him to respond wisely and effectively.

Temporal Discernment: He understands the spiritual significance of current events and cultural trends, maintaining proper perspective on temporal matters.

The Man of God in His Various Roles

The characteristics of a Man of God must be lived out through various roles and relationships. These roles provide practical contexts for demonstrating spiritual maturity and godly character.

The Man of God as Husband

In marriage, the Man of God demonstrates sacrificial love, servant leadership, and spiritual guidance. He creates an environment where his wife can flourish spiritually, emotionally, and personally.

Ephesians 5:25-26, TLV

"Husbands, love your wives, just as Christ also loved the church and gave Himself for her, that He might sanctify and cleanse her with the washing of water by the word."

This passage reveals that husbandly love should mirror Messiah's love for His people. This love is sacrificial, seeking the wife's spiritual development and personal well-being. The Man of God understands that his role is not to dominate but to serve, not to control but to nurture.

Practical expressions of this love include:

Spiritual Leadership: He leads family devotions, prayer, and worship, creating an atmosphere where spiritual growth can flourish.

Emotional Support: He provides a safe environment where his wife can express her thoughts, feelings, and concerns without judgment or criticism.

Physical Provision: He works diligently to provide for his family's material needs, understanding this as a divine responsibility.

Romantic Affection: He maintains romantic love and physical intimacy within the bounds of marriage, understanding that this strengthens the marital bond.

The Man of God as Father

As a father, the Man of God bears tremendous responsibility for his children's spiritual, emotional, and moral development. He understands that fatherhood is a divine calling requiring wisdom, patience, and consistent example.

Ephesians 6:4, TLV

"And you, fathers, do not provoke your children to wrath, but bring them up in the training and admonition of the Lord."

This verse presents both negative and positive aspects of fatherhood. The father must avoid provoking his children through harsh, inconsistent, or unreasonable treatment. Instead, he provides training (paideia) and instruction (nouthesia) that promotes spiritual growth and character development.

The Man of God demonstrates fatherhood through:

Consistent Discipline: He maintains consistent, loving discipline that teaches respect for authority and personal responsibility.

Spiritual Instruction: He teaches his children biblical principles, helping them understand God's character and ways.

Personal Example: He models the Messianic life through his own choices and responses, understanding that children learn more from observation than instruction.

Emotional Connection: He builds strong emotional bonds with his children, creating relationships that will endure throughout life.

The Man of God as Community Leader

Whether in formal leadership positions or informal influence, the Man of God serves as a positive force in his community. He seeks opportunities to serve others, promote justice, and demonstrate God's love through practical action.

Mattityahu 5:16, TLV

"Let your light so shine before men, that they may see your good works and glorify your Father in heaven."

This verse reveals that the Man of God's influence extends beyond his immediate family to the broader community. His good works should point others toward God rather than toward himself.

Community leadership manifests through:

Integrity in Business: He conducts all business dealings with complete honesty and fairness, treating employees, customers, and competitors with respect.

Civic Responsibility: He participates in community affairs, votes responsibly, and seeks to promote justice and righteousness in public policy.

Charitable Service: He gives generously to help those in need, understanding that practical service validates verbal testimony about God's love.

Mentoring Younger Men: He invests time and energy in developing the next generation of godly men, passing on wisdom and experience.

The Man of God as Kingdom Ambassador

Ultimately, the Man of God serves as an ambassador of God's kingdom, representing divine values and principles in a fallen world. This role requires courage, wisdom, and unwavering commitment to righteousness.

2 Corinthians 5:20, TLV

"Now then, we are ambassadors for Christ, as though God were pleading through us: we implore you on Christ's behalf, be reconciled to God."

An ambassador represents his home country's interests while living in foreign territory. The Man of God represents heaven's interests while living on earth, maintaining loyalty to divine principles even when they conflict with earthly wisdom.

This ambassadorial role involves:

Evangelistic Witness: He shares the gospel with those who don't know Messiah, understanding that eternal souls are at stake.

Prophetic Voice: He speaks biblical truth to cultural issues, even when such truth is unpopular or controversial.

Intercession: He prays for his community, nation, and world, understanding that prayer affects earthly events.

Cultural Influence: He seeks to influence culture toward biblical values through his work, relationships, and civic involvement.

The Eternal Perspective: Living with Kingdom Vision

The Man of God maintains constant awareness of eternity, understanding that this life is preparation for the next. This eternal perspective affects every decision, relationship, and priority, preventing him from becoming too attached to temporal things while motivating him toward eternal investment.

Colossians 3:2-3, TLV

"Set your mind on things above, not on things on the earth. For you died, and your life is hidden with Christ in God."

This verse reveals that the Man of God lives with dual citizenship—he is a citizen of heaven temporarily residing on earth. This perspective affects his values, priorities, and responses to circumstances.

The eternal perspective manifests through:

Eternal Values: He prioritizes spiritual growth, character development, and relationship with God over material accumulation or worldly success.

Eternal Relationships: He invests in relationships that have eternal significance, understanding that people are the only earthly treasure that will last forever.

Eternal Rewards: He works for eternal rewards rather than temporal recognition, understanding that his ultimate accountability is to God.

Eternal Hope: He maintains hope during difficult circumstances, understanding that present sufferings are temporary while future glory is eternal.

The Ongoing Transformation: A Lifetime Journey

Becoming a Man of God is not about achieving perfection but about submitting to ongoing divine transformation. It represents a lifetime journey of spiritual growth, character development, and increasing conformity to Messiah's image.

2 Corinthians 3:18, TLV

"But we all, with unveiled face, beholding as in a mirror the glory of the Lord, are being transformed into the same image from glory to glory, just as by the Spirit of the Lord."

This verse reveals that transformation is progressive—"from glory to glory"—indicating continuous spiritual development throughout life. The Man of God understands that he will never achieve perfection in this life but continues growing toward spiritual maturity. His perfection comes through Yeshua. And he understands that always.

This transformation involves:

Renewing the Mind: Through consistent Scripture study, he replaces worldly thinking patterns with biblical perspectives.

Strengthening the Spirit: Through prayer, worship, and spiritual disciplines, he develops spiritual strength and sensitivity.

Disciplining the Body: Through physical discipline and self-control, he maintains his body as a temple of the Holy Spirit.

Serving Others: Through practical service and ministry, he demonstrates God's love while developing spiritual maturity.

The Divine Calling: Answering God's Summons

The call to become a Man of God represents the highest honor available to any male. It transcends social status, economic position, educational achievement, or natural ability. God calls men from every background and circumstance, offering them the opportunity to participate in His eternal purposes.

The Weight of the Call

The divine summons to become a Man of God is not an invitation to religious performance but a radical reorientation of existence. It is a call to die—to ambitions, to self-sufficiency, to the world's definitions of success—so that the life of Messiah might be manifest in mortal flesh. The apostle Sha'ul (Paul) articulated this paradox with piercing clarity:

Galatians 2:20, TLV

"I have been crucified with Messiah; and it is no longer I who live, but Messiah lives in me. And the life I now live in the flesh, I live by faith in the Son of God, who loved me and gave Himself up for me."

This is the essence of the calling: a man emptied of self, yet filled with divine purpose; broken of pride, yet entrusted with heavenly authority. The Man of God does not merely know about God—he

32

knows God, intimately and unshakably, as Moses knew Him face to face, as David knew Him in the secret place, as Yeshua knew Him in the garden of surrender.

The Cost of the Mantle

History testifies that true men of God are forged in the furnace of adversity, not applauded in the arenas of cheap acclaim. Eliyahu (Elijah) emerged from the obscurity of Gilead to confront the prophets of Baal. Yirmeyahu (Jeremiah) bore the weight of divine words in a generation that despised his message. Yochanan the Immerser (John the Baptist) lived in the wilderness, a voice crying out, until his head was severed for the sake of truth.

The modern age, with its obsession with comfort and convenience, has produced a counterfeit version of this calling—a faith without fire, a discipleship without denial. But the true Man of God understands that the mantle comes at a price:

• The price of solitude—standing alone when the crowd chooses compromise.

• The price of suffering—enduring hardship as discipline from a loving Father.

• The price of surrender—relinquishing personal dreams to embrace a divine destiny.

The Promise of the Call

Yet, woven into this costly calling is an unbreakable promise: the presence of God. The Almighty does not summon a man to abandon him but to walk with him, as He walked with Enoch, as He spoke to Noah, as He strengthened Joshua. The Man of God is never alone, for the Ruach HaKodesh (Holy Spirit) dwells within him, guiding, correcting, and empowering him for every battle.

Joshua 1:9, TLV

"Have I not commanded you? Be strong and courageous! Do not be terrified or dismayed, for Adonai your God Is with you wherever you go."

This is the assurance that steels his resolve: Immanuel, God with us. Whether in the palace or the prison, in abundance or lack, in life or death—the presence of the Almighty transforms every circumstance into an opportunity for glory.

SYNOPSIS: The Essence of a Man of God

A Man of God is not defined by titles, robes, or the applause of men, but by the unmistakable imprint of the Divine upon his soul. He is a living paradox—weak, yet strong; humble, yet bold; broken, yet unshakable. He walks in the footsteps of the prophets, the apostles, and the Messiah Himself, carrying a message that comforts the afflicted and afflicts the comfortable.

He understands that the journey is not one of ascent to greatness but of descent into servanthood. The path is narrow, the cost is high, but the reward is eternal—a "well done" from the lips of the King of Kings.

In a world of shifting sands, he stands as a pillar of truth. In an age of moral fog, he burns as a lamp of righteousness. He is not perfect, but he is pursuing—straining toward the upward call, fighting the good fight, keeping the faith.

And when his earthly race is run, he will not leave behind monuments of stone but legacies of lives transformed, not by his might, but by the Spirit of the Living God who worked through him.

This is the Man of God. And this is only the beginning.

CHAPTER TWO: THE DIVINE CALL TO PROVISION

A Messianic Man's Sacred Responsibility

The Distorted Understanding of Provision

Contemporary society has reduced the sacred concept of provision to its most superficial elements—mere financial transactions, bill-paying obligations, or casual favors dispensed without thought or purpose. This reductionist perspective strips away the profound theological and relational depth inherent in the biblical understanding of what it means to be a provider. The Hebrew concept of provision encompasses far more than material sustenance; it embodies the very character of HaShem Himself, who provides for His creation with intentionality, love, and divine purpose.

The modern distortion has created a particularly troubling dynamic wherein segments of society—both male and female—have embraced shallow transactional relationships that bear no resemblance to the biblical model of covenant partnership. Many women have adopted a materialistic mindset that reduces masculine purpose to mere financial utility, failing to recognize that men are the architects and builders of civilization itself. Simultaneously, many men have abdicated their God-ordained roles, either through passive submission to cultural pressures or through an overreaction that swings toward domination rather than servant leadership.

This role confusion is not accidental but represents a deliberate assault by Satan against the divine order established at creation. The Adversary has masterfully orchestrated a reversal of biblical roles, creating confusion where God intended clarity, competition where He designed complementarity, and contempt where He established honor. In the original design, as recorded throughout Scripture, women eagerly embraced their calling to partner with and support their men, while men confidently assumed their responsibility to provide, protect, and lead with sacrificial love. This mutual submission to divine design created harmony and flourishing.

The contemporary cultural landscape reveals the devastating consequences of this role reversal. Men are no longer accorded the respect that their calling deserves, and truthfully, this reality stems partly from our own failures as men. We have allowed cultural pressures to reshape our understanding of masculinity, often swinging between extremes of passive acquiescence and aggressive dominance, neither of which reflects the biblical model of servant leadership. While it remains true that women have contributed to this cultural shift by embracing ideologies that diminish masculine value, men bear significant responsibility for allowing this transformation to occur without principled resistance grounded in Scripture.

The Hebrew Foundation of Provision

To understand the authentic meaning of being a provider, we must examine the original languages of Scripture. The Hebrew word nathan commonly translated as "to give" or "to provide," carries profound implications that extend far beyond mere material exchange. This word appears over 2,000 times in the Hebrew Scriptures, indicating its central importance to understanding God's character and His expectations for human relationships. The root concept encompasses the ideas of bestowing, placing, setting, appointing, and establishing—all suggesting intentional, purposeful action rather than casual or obligatory giving.

Similarly, the Hebrew kalkal means "to sustain" or "to maintain," while sharath conveys the concept of serving or ministering. These terms collectively paint a picture of provision that involves careful attention to needs, strategic resource allocation, and ongoing commitment to the welfare of others. The provider, in biblical terms, is one who observes, anticipates, and responds to needs with wisdom, generosity, and steadfast faithfulness.

The Aramaic and Greek texts of the New Testament continue this theme. The Greek word khorēgeō originally described the wealthy citizen who financed dramatic productions for the community's benefit, expecting no personal return but finding fulfillment in blessing others. The word diakoneō, meaning "to serve," emphasizes the servant-hearted nature of true provision. These linguistic foundations reveal that biblical provision always involves an element of sacrificial service, generous giving, and humble submission to God's purposes.

This understanding transforms the Messianic Man's approach to provision entirely. He recognizes that his role as provider extends far beyond his immediate household to encompass his broader community and, ultimately, the advancement of God's kingdom on earth. His provision becomes an act of worship, a practical demonstration of his understanding of divine character, and a testimony to the reality of God's own provisional nature.

The Cultural Crisis of Masculine Identity

The contemporary cultural landscape presents unique challenges for the Messianic Man seeking to fulfill his providential calling. Popular culture, particularly through entertainment media, has systematically undermined traditional expressions of masculine virtue. Musicians, actors, and social media influencers consistently promote narratives that reduce women to objects of sexual gratification while simultaneously emasculating men through the promotion of emotional instability, moral relativism, and spiritual emptiness.

This cultural programming has created a generation of young men who lack clear role models and foundational principles for understanding their divine calling. The concept of chivalry—once understood as the marriage of strength and gentleness, courage and courtesy—has been ridiculed as outdated or even oppressive. Yet chivalry, properly understood, represents nothing more than the practical application of biblical principles regarding how men should treat all people, particularly those who may be more vulnerable.

The tragic irony of our current cultural moment is that while many women loudly proclaim their independence and their lack of need for men, their actions and the broader social statistics reveal the opposite reality. The epidemic of anxiety, depression, and emotional instability among women in Western societies correlates directly with the breakdown of traditional family structures and the absence of strong, principled masculine leadership. Women desperately need men—not as oppressors or controllers, but as protectors, providers, and spiritual leaders who can offer stability, security, and godly direction.

Men, conversely, rarely engage in public declarations of independence from women, suggesting an intuitive understanding of the complementary nature of the sexes that many women have been conditioned to reject. This creates a complex dynamic for the Messianic Man, who must navigate between cultural hostility toward traditional masculine roles and the genuine need for his leadership and provision.

The Foundation of Masculine Confidence

The first step toward effective provision must begin with the Messianic Man's understanding of his identity in Messiah Yeshua. True masculine confidence cannot be manufactured through external achievements, social validation, or cultural conformity. Instead, it must be rooted in the unshakeable reality of God's indwelling presence through the Ruach HaKodesh (Holy Spirit).

Scripture declares that every believer is indwelt by the Spirit of the living God, and it is from this divine presence that authentic confidence emerges. This confidence manifests as biblical boldness—not arrogance or aggression, but the quiet assurance that comes from knowing one's identity, purpose, and calling in God's eternal plan. As it is written:

2 Timothy 1:7 TLV

For God has not given us a spirit of fear, but of power and love and sound judgment.

This divine empowerment enables the Messianic Man to function according to his created design rather than cultural expectations. Just as every element of creation has been designed with specific characteristics and purposes—the grasshopper does not attempt to bark like a dog, nor does the oak tree attempt to slither like a serpent—so men have been created with particular attributes and calling that distinguish them from women.

The observation of human civilization throughout history provides compelling evidence for the distinct contributions of masculine design. The great architectural achievements, infrastructure developments, technological innovations, and institutional frameworks that form the backbone of human society have predominantly emerged from masculine creativity, strength, and vision. This is not to diminish feminine contributions, which are equally vital but generally expressed in different spheres, but rather to affirm that masculine and feminine roles are complementary rather than identical.

The Adversary's strategy involves confusing this divine design through ideological movements that promote role reversal and gender confusion. Feminism, in its more radical expressions, seeks not merely equality of opportunity but the elimination of gender distinctions altogether. This ideological framework necessarily requires the diminishment of masculine authority and the elevation of feminine leadership in spheres where such leadership may not align with God's design.

Responding to Cultural Hostility with Biblical Wisdom

The Messianic Man must be prepared to encounter hostility when he attempts to fulfill his providential calling in contemporary society. Women who have been conditioned to view masculine courtesy as condescension or oppression may respond negatively to genuine expressions of chivalry and service. The natural human response to such rejection is either withdrawal or retaliation, both of which ultimately serve the Adversary's purposes by confirming negative stereotypes about masculine character.

Consider this common scenario: A Messianic Man approaches a restaurant door simultaneously with a woman. His natural inclination, informed by biblical principles of service and courtesy, leads him to open and hold the door for her. However, the woman responds with irritation, declaring, "I can open the door by myself, thank you," accompanied by a hostile expression that communicates offense rather than gratitude.

The carnal response would be immediate withdrawal coupled with defensive sarcasm: "Fine, go ahead and open the door yourself, then," followed by entering the restaurant while allowing the door to close behind him. This reaction, while understandable from a human perspective, represents capitulation to flesh rather than submission to Spirit-led wisdom.

Such responses inadvertently confirm the very stereotypes that hostile women hold regarding masculine character—that men are ultimately selfish, prideful, and retaliatory when their gestures are not appreciated. This creates a self-perpetuating cycle wherein masculine courtesy is rejected, men withdraw their courtesy, and women feel justified in their initial hostility.

The biblical alternative requires the Messianic Man to maintain his commitment to godly behavior regardless of the response he receives. Scripture provides clear guidance for such situations:

1 Peter 3:9 TLV

Do not repay evil for evil or insult for insult, but give a blessing instead—it is for this reason you were called, so that you might inherit a blessing.

This principle extends beyond mere passive non-retaliation to active blessing-giving in response to hostility. The Messianic Man recognizes that hostile responses often emerge from spiritual wounds, cultural conditioning, or demonic influence rather than personal animosity toward him specifically. His response must address the spiritual reality behind the natural circumstances.

In the door-holding scenario, the appropriate response might be: "I understand that you're capable of opening the door yourself. However, as a man who believes in God and seeks to honor Him through acts of service, I'd like to continue holding the door as a demonstration of my faith." This response accomplishes several objectives simultaneously: it affirms the woman's capability without surrendering the principle, it identifies the action as religiously motivated rather than condescending, it maintains masculine leadership without becoming defensive, and it potentially plants a seed that God might use to soften hearts toward both men and toward Himself.

Practical Applications of Providential Service

The scope of providential service extends far beyond courtesy gestures to encompass meaningful assistance that addresses genuine needs within the community. This includes financial assistance, practical help, volunteer service, and resource sharing—all motivated by the desire to reflect God's character and demonstrate His love for His creation.

James 1:27 TLV

Pure and undefiled religion before our God and Father is this: to care for orphans and widows in their distress, and to keep oneself unstained by the world.

41

The care of orphans and widows represents a fundamental biblical mandate that addresses populations particularly vulnerable to economic and social exploitation. In contemporary society, this principle extends to single mothers, elderly individuals without family support, disabled persons requiring assistance, and children in unstable family situations. The Messianic Man recognizes these individuals as specific objects of God's concern and therefore worthy of his practical investment.

Such provision might manifest through regular financial support for specific families, volunteer work with charitable organizations, professional services offered at reduced or no cost, or simple acts of practical assistance such as home maintenance, transportation, or meal preparation. The key is consistency, intentionality, and genuine care rather than sporadic or self-serving gestures.

Spiritual Provision Through Discipleship and Mentorship

The most significant provision a Messianic Man can offer extends beyond material assistance to encompass spiritual guidance, biblical instruction, and character development. In a culture increasingly devoid of strong masculine role models, particularly in spiritual matters, the need for authentic discipleship relationships has never been more acute.

Matthew 28:19-20 TLV

Go therefore and make disciples of all nations, immersing them in the name of the Father and the Son and the Ruach ha-Kodesh, and teaching them to observe all that I have commanded you. And remember! I am with you always, even to the end of the age.

The Great Commission represents not merely an evangelistic mandate but a comprehensive discipleship responsibility that includes ongoing spiritual formation and biblical instruction. The Messianic Man recognizes that many pastors and religious leaders have compromised biblical truth through accommodation to cultural pressures, leaving young people without authentic spiritual guidance.

Male discipleship carries particular importance because boys and young men naturally seek masculine models for behavior, decision-making, and character development. A father's influence remains primary, but many children grow up without consistent masculine presence, creating opportunities for godly men to fill this void through mentorship relationships.

Effective spiritual provision requires several key elements:

Consistent Biblical Study: The Messianic Man must maintain regular engagement with Scripture, not merely for personal edification but to ensure his ability to provide accurate biblical guidance to others. As Paul instructs Timothy:

2 Timothy 2:15 TLV

Make every effort to present yourself before God as tried and true, a worker unashamed, cutting straight the word of truth.

Strategic Communication: Every conversation represents an opportunity to plant spiritual seeds or provide biblical perspective on life circumstances. This requires careful attention to word choice, timing, and spiritual sensitivity rather than forced or inappropriate religious commentary.

Intercessory Prayer: Effective spiritual provision includes regular prayer for those within the Messianic Man's sphere of influence. This might involve maintaining prayer lists, dedicating specific times for intercession, and seeking God's guidance regarding practical ways to serve others.

1 Timothy 2:1-4 TLV

First of all, then, I urge that requests, prayers, intercessions, and thanksgiving be made for all people—for kings and all who are in authority, so that we might live a tranquil and quiet life in all godliness

43

and dignity. This is good and acceptable before God our Savior, who wants all people to be saved and to come to the knowledge of the truth.

Scriptural Encouragement: The ability to provide relevant biblical encouragement during times of crisis, decision-making, or spiritual struggle requires familiarity with Scripture and sensitivity to individual needs.

Hebrews 10:24-25 TLV

And let us consider how to stir up one another to love and good deeds—not neglecting our own meeting together, as is the habit of some, but encouraging each other, and all the more as you see the Day approaching.

Emotional Provision Through Presence and Support

Contemporary society has created unprecedented levels of emotional instability, anxiety, and relational dysfunction. Many people struggle with depression, loneliness, and purposelessness, often lacking the emotional support systems that previous generations enjoyed through extended family networks and stable community relationships.

The Messianic Man's emotional provision addresses these needs through several practical applications:

Active Presence During Crisis: Physical presence during times of grief, illness, financial difficulty, or family crisis communicates care and support more effectively than words alone. This might involve adjusting personal schedules, traveling distances, or making financial sacrifices to be available when needed.

Romans 12:15 TLV

Rejoice with those who rejoice; weep with those who weep.

Encouraging Communication: The power of affirming words cannot be overstated in a culture that tends toward criticism and negativity. Simple expressions such as "You're doing excellent work," "Your friendship means a great deal to me," or "I see God using you in significant ways" can provide emotional strength that sustains individuals through difficult periods.

Ephesians 4:29 TLV

Let no unwholesome word come out of your mouth, but only what is good for building others up according to the need, so that it gives grace to those who hear.

Biblical Counseling: Many emotional struggles stem from spiritual issues, wrong thinking patterns, or lack of biblical perspective on life circumstances. The Messianic Man equipped with scriptural knowledge can provide counsel that addresses root causes rather than mere symptoms.

Proverbs 11:14 TLV

Where there is no guidance, a people falls, but in abundance of counselors there is safety.

Creating Safe Environments: The Messianic Man's presence should create an atmosphere where others feel secure enough to share burdens, express concerns, and seek guidance without fear of judgment or betrayal. This requires maintaining confidentiality, avoiding gossip, and demonstrating consistent character that builds trust over time.

Physical Provision Through Charitable Action

The most visible expression of providential character involves meeting tangible needs through financial assistance, practical help, and resource sharing. This type of provision requires wisdom, discernment, and strategic thinking to ensure maximum effectiveness while avoiding the creation of unhealthy dependencies.

Proverbs 19:17 TLV

One who is gracious to the poor lends to Adonai, and He will repay him for his good deed.

Effective physical provision might include:

Strategic Charitable Giving: Rather than random or emotional giving, the Messianic Man seeks God's guidance regarding when, where, and how much to give. This might involve paying for someone's groceries, covering medical expenses, providing transportation, or offering interest-free loans for emergency situations.

Volunteer Service: Donating time and labor through organizations that serve the poor, elderly, or disadvantaged provides direct physical assistance while demonstrating kingdom values.

James 2:15-16 TLV

If a brother or sister is naked and lacks daily food, and one of you says to them, "Go in shalom, keep warm and well fed," but you do not give them what the body needs, what good is that?

Employment Opportunities: Business owners or individuals in hiring positions can provide physical provision to believers through employment opportunities, particularly for those struggling economically or seeking to rebuild their lives after difficult circumstances.

Leviticus 25:35 TLV

Now if your brother becomes poor and cannot maintain himself among you, you are to support him like a stranger or temporary resident, so he can live among you.

Hospitality: Opening one's home for meals, temporary lodging, or fellowship gatherings addresses both physical and emotional needs while creating opportunities for spiritual influence.

Hebrews 13:2 TLV

Do not neglect hospitality to strangers, for by doing so some have entertained angels without knowing it.

The Wisdom of Discernment in Provision

Yeshua's instruction to His disciples provides essential guidance for the Messianic Man's approach to provision in a complex and often hostile world:

Matthew 10:16 TLV

Behold, I am sending you out as sheep in the midst of wolves, so be wise as serpents and innocent as doves.

This balance between wisdom and innocence, shrewdness and purity, requires careful discernment in all providential activities. The Messianic Man must avoid both naïve vulnerability that enables exploitation and cynical suspicion that prevents genuine ministry. This discernment develops through prayer, biblical study, and experience gained through faithful service over time.

Practical wisdom in provision includes:

Evaluating Genuine Need: Distinguishing between authentic necessity and manipulation or laziness requires careful observation and sometimes direct investigation.

Setting Appropriate Boundaries: Healthy provision establishes limits that prevent enabling destructive behaviors while maintaining openness to legitimate needs.

Seeking Divine Guidance: Each situation requires prayer and spiritual sensitivity to determine appropriate responses that align with God's purposes.

Maintaining Personal Integrity: All provision must be conducted with complete honesty, appropriate accountability, and careful stewardship of resources.

Biblical Examples of Failed Provision: The Case of Nabal

The account of Nabal in 1 Samuel 25 provides a sobering example of how wealth and opportunity can be squandered through selfishness, pride, and spiritual blindness. Nabal's name itself means "fool," and his behavior perfectly exemplifies the biblical definition of foolishness—not lack of intelligence, but willful disregard for God and His ways.

Psalm 53:2 TLV

The fool says in his heart: "There is no God." They are corrupt, commit vile injustice. There is no one who does good.

Nabal possessed significant wealth—3,000 sheep and 1,000 goats—along with extensive business operations that required protection from bandits and raiders. David and his men had provided this protection faithfully, asking for nothing in return except occasional food and supplies. When David's messengers approached Nabal during shearing season—traditionally a time of celebration and generosity—requesting modest provisions, Nabal's response revealed his character:

1 Samuel 25:10-11 TLV

But Nabal answered David's servants by saying, "Who is David? And who is Jesse's son? Nowadays there are many slaves each running away from his master. So should I take my bread, my water and my meat that I have cooked for my shearers, and give it to men whom I don't know where they come from?"

Nabal's failure demonstrates several critical errors that the Messianic Man must carefully avoid:

Ingratitude: Despite receiving valuable protection services, Nabal refused to acknowledge the benefit he had received or express any appreciation for David's assistance.

Selfishness: Although abundantly blessed with resources, Nabal hoarded his wealth rather than sharing with those who had served him faithfully.

Spiritual Blindness: Nabal failed to recognize God's hand in his prosperity or his responsibility to use his blessings for others' benefit.

Pride and Arrogance: His dismissive attitude toward David revealed contempt for those he considered beneath his social status, despite their service to him.

Short-sighted Foolishness: Nabal's refusal to provide modest assistance created a life-threatening crisis that required his wife's intervention to prevent disaster.

The contrast between Nabal and his wife Abigail provides additional insight into proper providential character. When Abigail learned of her husband's insulting response to David's request, she immediately took action to rectify the situation:

1 Samuel 25:18-19 TLV

Then Abigail hurried and took 200 loaves, two bottles of wine, five dressed sheep, five measures of roasted corn, 100 cakes of raisins, and 200 cakes of figs, and put them on donkeys. Then she said to her young men, "Go on ahead of me—see, I am coming after you." But she did not tell her husband Nabal.

Abigail's response demonstrated wisdom, generosity, humility, and urgent action to address a crisis created by her husband's foolishness. Her intervention saved not only David from committing violence but also preserved her household from destruction. God's subsequent judgment on Nabal and blessing on Abigail (who later became David's wife) confirms the importance of generous, wise provision versus selfish hoarding. Honestly, find a wife like Abigail.

Biblical Examples of Excellent Provision: The Life of Joseph

Joseph's life provides perhaps the most comprehensive biblical example of providential leadership that extends beyond family boundaries to encompass entire nations and peoples. His story

49

demonstrates how God can use one faithful man to provide for countless others during times of extreme crisis.

Genesis 41:16 TLV

Joseph answered Pharaoh, saying, "It is not in me. God will give Pharaoh a favorable answer."

Joseph's approach to provision encompassed multiple dimensions:

Spiritual Provision Through Divine Revelation: Joseph's ability to interpret dreams and discern God's will provided spiritual guidance during times of uncertainty. His consistent attribution of this ability to God rather than personal wisdom demonstrated humility while pointing others toward divine truth.

When Pharaoh experienced troubling dreams about impending famine, Joseph not only interpreted the dreams but provided a comprehensive strategy for national survival:

Genesis 41:33-36 TLV

So now let Pharaoh select a man discerning and wise, and set him over the land of Egypt. Let Pharaoh do this: appoint overseers over the land, and take a fifth of the produce of the land of Egypt during the seven years of abundance. Let them gather all the food of these good years that are coming, and store grain under Pharaoh's authority for food in the cities, and preserve it. The food will be a reserve for the land during the seven years of famine that will come over the land of Egypt, so that the land will not perish during the famine.

Physical Provision Through Strategic Planning: Joseph's administrative abilities enabled him to implement a massive food storage and distribution system that saved Egypt and surrounding nations from starvation. His foresight, organizational skills, and commitment to stewardship created the infrastructure necessary for survival during seven years of severe famine.

Genesis 41:56-57 TLV

When the famine was over all the surface of the earth, Joseph opened all the storehouses and sold to the Egyptians, for the famine was severe in the land of Egypt. All countries came into Egypt to Joseph to buy grain, because the famine was severe in all the earth.

Emotional Provision Through Forgiveness and Reconciliation: Perhaps most remarkably, Joseph extended emotional healing to his own family despite their previous betrayal. When his brothers came to Egypt seeking food, Joseph tested their character before revealing his identity, then offered complete forgiveness coupled with theological perspective on their past actions.

Genesis 45:5-8 TLV

So now, don't be grieved and don't be angry in your own eyes that you sold me here—since it was for preserving life that God sent me here before you. For these two years the famine has been in the land, and there are yet five years in which there will be neither plowing nor harvest. God sent me before you to preserve for you a remnant in the earth, and to keep you alive for a great deliverance. So then, it was not you who sent me here, but God, and He has made me a father to Pharaoh, lord of all his household, and ruler over all the land of Egypt.

Joseph's response demonstrates several key principles for the Messianic Man:

Divine Perspective on Suffering: Joseph recognized God's sovereignty in allowing difficult circumstances that ultimately served providential purposes.

Commitment to Blessing Rather than Revenge: Despite having the power to punish his brothers, Joseph chose to provide for them and their families.

51

Stewardship of Leadership Positions: Joseph used his governmental authority to serve others rather than enrich himself or settle personal scores.

Integration of Faith and Practical Action: Joseph combined trust in God with diligent work, careful planning, and wise decision-making.

The Messianic Standard of Provision

The ultimate model for providential living remains Yeshua Himself, whose earthly ministry demonstrated perfect integration of spiritual, emotional, and physical provision for those around Him. His approach provides the definitive template for the Messianic Man's service to others.

Matthew 9:35-36 TLV

Yeshua was going around all the towns and villages, teaching in their synagogues and proclaiming the Good News of the kingdom, and healing every kind of disease and sickness. When He saw the crowds, He felt compassion for them because they were harassed and helpless, like sheep without a shepherd.

Yeshua's ministry consistently addressed human needs at multiple levels simultaneously. His teaching provided spiritual nourishment and divine truth. His healing addressed physical ailments and disabilities. His compassionate presence offered emotional comfort and hope. His willingness to associate with outcasts and sinners provided social inclusion and dignity.

The Messianic Man seeks to emulate this comprehensive approach to provision, recognizing that human beings have complex needs that require multifaceted responses. He avoids the error of addressing only physical needs while ignoring spiritual poverty, or focusing exclusively on spiritual matters while remaining indifferent to practical struggles.

Luke 4:18-19 TLV

"The Ruach Adonai is upon Me, because He has anointed Me to proclaim Good News to the poor. He has sent Me to proclaim release to the captives and recovery of sight to the blind, to set free the oppressed, and to proclaim the year of Adonai's favor."

This mission statement encompasses social justice, spiritual liberation, physical healing, and economic relief—all integrated into a coherent ministry of comprehensive provision.

Practical Implementation in Contemporary Context

The Messianic Man living in contemporary society faces unique challenges in implementing biblical principles of provision while navigating cultural hostility, legal constraints, and economic limitations. However, these obstacles need not prevent faithful service when approached with wisdom and creativity.

Starting with Personal Character: All external provision must flow from internal spiritual formation. The Messianic Man prioritizes his relationship with God, regular biblical study, consistent prayer, and accountability relationships that support his spiritual growth.

Developing Practical Skills: Effective provision often requires specific competencies—financial knowledge, counseling abilities, practical skills, or professional expertise that enables meaningful assistance to others.

Building Community Networks: Isolated individuals have limited capacity for significant provision. The Messianic Man cultivates relationships with like-minded believers who can collaborate in serving others more effectively than individual efforts alone.

Seeking Divine Guidance: Each opportunity for provision requires prayer and spiritual discernment to determine appropriate responses that align with God's purposes and timing.

Maintaining Long-term Perspective: Effective provision often requires sustained commitment over extended periods rather than sporadic or emotional responses to immediate needs.

A Story of Divine Provision:

One day, within a neighborhood stricken by poverty in the deep South, a young woman of approximately twenty-three years old lived in hardship with her much older mother. They possessed little, and her mother depended entirely upon her daughter's modest income to sustain their basic needs—rent, utilities, and the essentials of survival. She labored eight grueling hours, five days a week, at a local fast-food establishment down the street, a journey that required precious bus fare for the twice-daily commute. This had been her reality for nearly three years, each day blending into the next in an endless cycle of work and worry. Some days, when she gets off work just a few short minutes later than usual, she would miss the final bus which meant she would have to walk the extensive journey.

Then, unexpectedly, an old friend she hadn't spoken to in months called. Her face registered confusion upon seeing the familiar number, immediately recalling how this friend would persistently invite her to attend the Messianic Jewish congregation on Shabbat mornings. She had always declined these invitations, offering vague promises of "someday" that never seemed to arrive. It had been months since their last conversation.

She answered the phone hesitantly, perhaps hoping it might go to voicemail instead. Surprisingly, the conversation flowed naturally and warmly. But then came the familiar question.

"When are you going to come to my synagogue?" her friend inquired with genuine sincerity.

She sighed deeply before responding, "I suppose. . .I could try this Saturday."

That weekend marked the beginning of an extraordinary transformation. As she stepped into the modest synagogue building, she was immediately embraced by a warmth she had never experienced. The congregation welcomed her not as a stranger, but as family. Week after week, she found herself returning, drawn by something she couldn't quite articulate—a sense of belonging, of being truly seen and valued.

What she didn't know was that the elders had taken notice of her circumstances, specifically because of her friend making them aware of her situation. They observed her worn clothing, her tired countenance after long shifts, and the way she carefully counted bus fare each week. More importantly, they witnessed her hunger for spiritual truth and her genuine heart for God's word. In quiet meetings after services, they began discussing how they might demonstrate God's provision in her life.

For three months, while she grew in faith and fellowship, the elders orchestrated something remarkable. Each member of the leadership contributed faithfully to a special fund, their hearts moved by her dedication despite her obvious financial struggles. They researched reliable vehicles, consulted mechanics, and prayed over their decision. Their goal was not merely charity, but a tangible expression of God's faithfulness to those who seek Him.

On the third month anniversary of her first visit, after the Shabbat service had concluded and most congregants had departed, the elders asked her to remain for a moment. Her friend stood nearby, barely containing her excitement.

"We've been watching your faithfulness," the head elder began gently. "Your commitment to worship despite your circumstances has blessed us all. We believe God has called us to be instruments of His provision in your life."

They led her outside to the parking lot, where a pristine 2014 sedan sat gleaming in the afternoon sun, a large bow adorning its roof. Keys dangled from the elder's weathered hand.

"This belongs to you," he said simply. "Paid in full. A gift from your spiritual family."

The young woman's composure crumbled as tears streamed down her face. Her hands trembled as she covered her mouth in disbelief. For three months, while she had been learning to trust God's word, this congregation had been proving His faithfulness through their actions. They had saved diligently, sacrificially, moved by a divine calling to demonstrate that God's people need not lack when the body of believers operates as it was designed.

"I don't understand," she whispered through her tears.

"You don't need to understand," the elder replied with a knowing smile. "You just need to receive. This is how provision works in the Kingdom—not through our own striving, but through God's people responding to His heart for one another."

As she held those keys in her trembling hands, she realized she was witnessing something far greater than generous charity. This was a living demonstration of biblical community, where believers' needs become opportunities for others to participate in God's provision. The congregation hadn't just given her transportation; they had shown her what it means to be part of a family that reflects Heaven's economics.

That evening, as she drove home in her new car—no longer dependent on bus schedules or fare—she understood that her three months of faithful attendance had been met by three months of faithful preparation. The synagogue had exemplified provision not through mere words, but through coordinated action, sacrificial giving, and the recognition that God's abundance flows through willing vessels.

The vehicle had opened up doors for her to find work within places she would consider far before her reception of the blessing.

To this day, she still attends the synagogue and has used the surplus of income from her new job to feed her congregations growth.

Her story became a testimony that spread throughout their community: when believers gather with pure hearts and open hands, provision manifests in ways that surpass human understanding, demonstrating that faith and community remain God's chosen instruments for meeting the needs of His people.

Conclusion: The Call to Sacrificial Service

The role of provider represents far more than cultural expectation or social obligation—it embodies the very heart of masculine calling as designed by the Creator. The Messianic Man who embraces this calling participates in the ongoing work of tikkun olam—repairing the world—through practical expressions of divine love and concern.

Philippians 2:3-4 TLV

Do nothing out of selfishness or conceit, but with humility consider others as more important than yourselves—looking out not only for your own interests, but also for the interests of others.

This providential calling requires the integration of spiritual depth, emotional maturity, and practical wisdom. It demands the courage to serve in a culture that may misunderstand or reject such service. It necessitates the humility to give without expectation of recognition or reward. It calls for the perseverance to continue serving even when responses are disappointing or hostile.

The contemporary world desperately needs men who understand and embrace this biblical vision of masculine purpose. Families are disintegrating for lack of strong, faithful providers. Communities are fragmenting due to the absence of servant leaders. Entire societies are suffering from the deficit of men who will assume responsibility for the welfare of others without expecting personal benefit.

The question facing every man who claims faith in Messiah Yeshua is whether he will answer this call to providential service or continue to allow cultural pressures to diminish his understanding of masculine purpose. The stakes could not be higher—not only for his own spiritual development but for the countless individuals whose lives might be transformed through his faithful service.

Isaiah 58:10-11 TLV

If you extend your soul to the hungry, and satisfy the afflicted soul, then your light will rise in darkness and your gloom will become like noonday. Adonai will guide you continually, satisfy your soul in drought, and give strength to your bones. You will be like a watered garden, like a spring of water, whose waters do not fail.

The promise remains as relevant today as when originally given—the man who commits himself to serving others according to biblical principles will experience divine blessing, guidance, and fulfillment that no worldly achievement can provide. This is the heritage of the Messianic Man who understands his calling as provider: not merely to pay bills or dispense favors, but to sustain, serve, and sacrifice for the advancement of God's kingdom on earth.

The choice stands before every man: Will you embrace the sacred responsibility of provision as designed by your Creator, or will you surrender to cultural pressures that diminish masculine purpose to mere financial utility? The answer to this question will determine not only the trajectory of your own life but the legacy you leave for future generations.

Joshua 24:15 TLV

If it seems wrong in your eyes to serve Adonai, then choose for yourselves today whom you will serve... But as for me and my household, we will serve Adonai.

The call to provision is ultimately a call to service—service to God through service to His people. May every Messianic Man who reads these words find the courage to answer this call with the same commitment demonstrated by Joshua, Joseph, and ultimately by

Yeshua Himself. The world awaits men who will provide not out of obligation but out of love, not from compulsion but from compassion, not for recognition but for the advancement of righteousness.

This is the way of the Messianic Man. This is the path of the biblical provider. This is the calling that awaits your response.

CHAPTER THREE: THE MESSIANIC MAN AS PROTECTOR

2 Thessalonians 3:3, TLV
"But ADONAI is faithful; He will establish you and guard you from the evil one."

The World's Counterfeit Vision of Protection

In our contemporary society, the concept of masculine protection has been distorted through a lens that emphasizes external manifestations over internal spiritual reality. This worldly paradigm reduces the sacred calling of protection to mere physical or material dimensions, creating a shallow foundation that inevitably crumbles under the weight of life's genuine challenges.

The modern world defines a protector through several superficial criteria that, while containing elements of truth, fall woefully short of God's divine standard. Physical prowess and aggressive behavior are often mistaken for true protection. Society celebrates the boxer, the wrestler, the martial artist—those who can physically dominate others—as natural protectors. Yet Scripture teaches us that *"the battle is ADONAI's" (1 Samuel 17:47, TLV)*, and that genuine protection flows from spiritual strength rather than muscular force.

Financial provision has become perhaps the most pervasive counterfeit of biblical protection in our materialistic age. Men are measured by their earning capacity, their ability to provide luxury, their financial portfolio. Women, influenced by this worldly mindset, often seek men based on their economic potential rather than their spiritual maturity. This creates unions built on sand rather than rock, marriages that collapse when economic storms arise because they lack the spiritual foundation that can weather any trial.

The world also glorifies dramatic acts of heroism—the firefighter who rescues someone from a burning building, the soldier who throws himself on a grenade, the civilian who stops a robbery. While such acts may indeed reflect courage and selflessness, they represent only momentary expressions of protection rather than the consistent, daily commitment that true biblical protection requires. A man may perform one heroic act and still fail miserably in his ongoing responsibility to guard those under his care.

Perhaps most destructive is the worldly confusion between protection and domination. In cultures that misunderstand masculine authority, men who control, manipulate, or intimidate others are perceived as protective. This represents a complete inversion of biblical truth, where protection flows from servant leadership, not tyrannical control. The Messianic Man understands that true authority comes through laying down one's life for others, following the pattern established by Yeshua Himself.

Finally, the mere possession of weapons or occupation in security-related fields is often equated with protective capability. While such tools and roles may serve legitimate purposes, they cannot substitute for the spiritual qualities that define genuine protection: wisdom, discernment, moral courage, and above all, submission to the God of Israel.

These counterfeit forms of protection share a common deficiency: they focus on human strength rather than divine empowerment, on external appearances rather than internal transformation, on temporal security rather than eternal significance. They fail to recognize that true protection is fundamentally a spiritual calling that requires spiritual resources.

The Biblical Foundation of Protection

When we examine the Hebrew Scriptures, we discover that the concept of protection is woven throughout the fabric of God's relationship with His people. The primary Hebrew word for protection, shamar, appears over 450 times in the Tanakh, conveying the idea of guarding, keeping watch, preserving, and maintaining vigilance. This word encompasses far more than defensive action; it implies proactive care, constant attention, and loving vigilance.

God Himself is portrayed as the ultimate protector of Israel: *"He who watches over Israel neither slumbers nor sleeps. ADONAI is your keeper; ADONAI is your shade at your right hand"* **(Psalm 121:4-5, TLV)**. The Messianic Man, created in God's image, is called to reflect this divine attribute in his relationships with others. Just as God watches over Israel with unwavering attention, the Messianic Man maintains constant vigilance over those entrusted to his care.

The role of protector extends beyond mere physical defense to encompass spiritual, emotional, and moral guardianship. This comprehensive understanding of protection reflects the holistic nature of biblical anthropology, which recognizes that human beings are integrated beings requiring care for body, soul, and spirit.

Scripture presents protection not as an option for men but as a divine mandate. *"But if anyone does not provide for his own, especially his household, he has denied the faith and is worse than an unbeliever" (1 Timothy 5:8, TLV)*. The Greek word "pronoeo" used here means to think ahead, to provide for in advance, suggesting that protection involves anticipatory care rather than merely reactive response.

The Messianic Man's role as protector finds its ultimate expression in his relationship with the God of Israel. He cannot effectively guard others unless he first submits to God's protective authority over his own life. This submission is not weakness but wisdom, recognizing that human strength is insufficient for the spiritual battles that define our existence.

The Spiritual Dimension of Protection

The most critical aspect of the Messianic Man's protective role operates in the spiritual realm. This dimension of protection directly impacts the eternal destiny of those under his care and requires the highest level of spiritual maturity and commitment.

Leading Through Intercessory Prayer

The Messianic Man understands that his primary weapon in spiritual warfare is prayer. Like Job, who *"would rise early in the morning and offer burnt offerings according to the number of them all. For Job said, 'Perhaps my children have sinned and cursed God in their hearts.' Job did this continually"* *(Job 1:5, TLV)*, the spiritual protector maintains constant intercession for those he guards.

This intercessory ministry requires discipline and sacrifice. The Messianic Man rises early, stays up late, and interrupts his schedule to bring his family and community before the throne of grace. He prays not only for their immediate needs but for their spiritual growth, their protection from temptation, their deepening relationship with God, and their eternal destiny.

Teaching and Transmitting Truth

The commandment given to Israel applies equally to the Messianic Man: *"These words, which I am commanding you today, shall be on your heart. You are to teach them diligently to your children, and speak of them when you sit in your house, when you walk by the way, when you lie down and when you rise up"* *(Deuteronomy 6:6-7, TLV)*.

Spiritual protection requires more than defensive measures; it demands proactive instruction in righteousness. The Messianic Man becomes a teacher, interpreter, and guide, helping others understand

God's word and apply it to their lives. He doesn't simply quote Scripture but explains its meaning, demonstrates its application, and lives out its principles in daily life.

This teaching ministry extends beyond formal instruction to include correction and discipline. The Messianic Man must have the courage to confront sin, address error, and guide others toward repentance when necessary. This requires great wisdom and love, correcting in such a way that restores rather than destroys.

Standing Against Spiritual Deception

In our age of spiritual confusion, the Messianic Man must be equipped to identify and counter false teachings, deceptive philosophies, and ungodly influences that threaten those under his care. He studies Scripture diligently, not merely for personal edification but to become a skilled defender of truth.

This protective role requires discernment to distinguish between legitimate spiritual growth and dangerous deviation. The Messianic Man must be familiar with the tactics of the enemy, understanding how Satan operates to deceive and destroy. He maintains vigilance against subtle compromises that can lead to spiritual shipwreck.

Modeling Spiritual Maturity

Perhaps the most powerful form of spiritual protection is the example of a life fully surrendered to God. The Messianic Man protects others by demonstrating what it means to walk in faith, to trust God in difficult circumstances, to maintain integrity under pressure, and to love sacrificially.

This modeling extends to his prayer life, his study of Scripture, his worship, his relationships, and his response to trials. Others observe his life and gain courage to face their own spiritual battles because they see the reality of God's power working through him.

The Physical Dimension of Protection

While spiritual protection takes precedence, the Messianic Man also bears responsibility for the physical welfare of those under his care. This aspect of protection requires both courage and wisdom, strength and gentleness.

Defending Against Physical Threats

The Messianic Man must be prepared to physically defend his family and community when necessary. This doesn't mean he seeks conflict or acts aggressively, but he remains ready to interpose himself between his loved ones and any threat to their safety.

Scripture provides numerous examples of righteous men who took up arms to protect others. Abraham pursued the kings who had captured Lot, taking 318 trained men to rescue his nephew *(Genesis 14:14-16)*. Moses defended the daughters of Reuel from shepherds who were harassing them *(Exodus 2:17)*. David's mighty men risked their lives repeatedly to protect their king and their people.

The Messianic Man trains himself physically, not out of pride or aggression, but out of love for those he protects. He maintains his body as a temple of the Holy Spirit, keeping himself in condition to respond effectively when physical protection is needed.

Providing Material Needs

Physical protection extends beyond defense to include provision. The Messianic Man works diligently to ensure that his family has adequate food, shelter, clothing, and other necessities. This provision flows from love rather than mere obligation, reflecting God's faithful provision for His people.

This responsibility requires planning, hard work, and sometimes sacrifice. The Messianic Man may need to work long hours, take on additional responsibilities, or forego personal pleasures to ensure his family's needs are met. He approaches this work as ministry, understanding that faithful provision is a form of worship.

Creating Safe Environments

The Messianic Man takes responsibility for creating and maintaining environments where his family can flourish. This includes ensuring their physical safety through proper maintenance of their home, appropriate security measures, and careful attention to potential hazards.

He also creates emotional safety by maintaining order, establishing clear boundaries, and ensuring that his home is a place of peace rather than conflict. He doesn't rule through fear or intimidation but through consistent, loving leadership that creates stability and security.

The Emotional Dimension of Protection

The emotional aspect of protection may be the most challenging for many men, requiring sensitivity, patience, and emotional intelligence that doesn't always come naturally to masculine temperament.

Providing Emotional Stability

The Messianic Man serves as an emotional anchor for his family, providing stability during storms and certainty during times of confusion. He doesn't allow his emotions to control his actions but responds to emotional situations with wisdom and calm strength.

This stability comes from his relationship with God rather than from his own emotional state. Even when he feels uncertain or anxious, he maintains his trust in God's faithfulness, providing a model of faith that others can follow.

Creating Emotional Safety

Emotional protection requires creating an environment where family members feel safe to express their thoughts and feelings without fear of ridicule, rejection, or retaliation. The Messianic Man listens attentively, validates emotions even when he doesn't agree with the conclusions drawn from them, and responds with patience and understanding.

He guards his words carefully, understanding that "death and life are in the power of the tongue." (Proverbs 18:21, TLV). He speaks words that build up rather than tear down, that encourage rather than discourage, that bring hope rather than despair.

Confronting Threats to Emotional Well-being

The Messianic Man protects his family from emotional harm by confronting bullies, addressing unhealthy relationships, and standing against anyone who would emotionally abuse or manipulate those under his care. He doesn't allow others to speak destructively to his family members or to undermine their emotional well-being.

This protection extends to helping family members develop healthy boundaries, teaching them to recognize and respond to emotional manipulation, and giving them tools to protect themselves when he's not present.

The Example of Yeshua: The Ultimate Protector

The life and ministry of Yeshua HaMashiach provides the perfect model for understanding the role of protector. Every aspect of His earthly ministry demonstrated sacrificial protection of those He came to save.

Healing as Protection

Yeshua's healing ministry was fundamentally an act of protection, delivering people from the ravages of disease, demon possession, and spiritual oppression. When He healed the man with the withered hand on Shabbat *(Mark 3:1-6, TLV)*, He demonstrated that protecting and restoring human life takes precedence over rigid religious tradition.

His healings weren't merely displays of divine power but acts of compassionate protection, restoring people to wholeness and freeing them from conditions that threatened their well-being. The Messianic Man follows this example by seeking opportunities to bring healing and restoration to those around him.

Confronting Evil as Protection

Yeshua regularly confronted evil forces that threatened the people He came to save. His exorcisms were acts of protection, delivering people from spiritual oppression and demonic influence. When He cast out Legion from the Gerasene demoniac *(Mark 5:1-20, TLV)*, He demonstrated the power of God to protect people from the most severe spiritual attacks.

The Messianic Man follows this example by courageously confronting evil in all its forms, whether spiritual, moral, or social. He doesn't ignore or tolerate evil but stands against it with the authority and power that God provides.

Teaching as Protection

Yeshua's teaching ministry was fundamentally protective, guarding people from spiritual deception and leading them into truth. His parables, sermons, and private instruction all served to protect people from the lies of the enemy and the false teachings of religious leaders.

The Messianic Man protects through teaching, ensuring that those under his care understand God's truth and are equipped to discern error. He doesn't merely transmit information but helps others develop spiritual discernment and wisdom.

Sacrificial Death as Ultimate Protection

Yeshua's death on the cross represents the ultimate act of protection, as He gave His life to save humanity from sin, death, and eternal judgment. *"Greater love has no one than this: that he lay down his life for his friends" (John 15:13, TLV).* This sacrificial love defines the heart of true protection.

The Messianic Man follows this example by being willing to sacrifice his own interests, comfort, and even his life for the sake of those he protects. This doesn't mean he seeks martyrdom, but he holds his own life lightly when compared to the welfare of those entrusted to his care.

A Failed Example: The Protective Facade

Consider Marcus, a man who appeared to embody many of society's ideals of masculine protection. He was physically imposing, standing six feet four inches tall with a muscular build developed through years of weightlifting and mixed martial arts training. His career as a corporate executive provided substantial financial resources, allowing him to live in an affluent neighborhood and send his children to private schools. By worldly standards, he was the epitome of a successful protector.

Yet beneath this impressive exterior, Marcus failed fundamentally in his God-given role as protector. His physical strength became a source of intimidation rather than security for his family. When angry, he would raise his voice and loom over his wife and children, using his size to control rather than protect. His martial arts training made him proud and aggressive, quick to resolve conflicts through force rather than wisdom.

His financial success became his primary identity, and he used his wealth to control his family's behavior. He would withhold money as punishment and provide expensive gifts as rewards, creating a transactional relationship rather than one based on love and trust. His wife felt like an employee rather than a partner, and his children learned to fear his displeasure rather than respect his authority.

Spiritually, Marcus was a desert. He rarely prayed, studied Scripture sporadically, and attended church only when it served his social or business interests. When his family faced spiritual challenges, he was unprepared and unequipped to provide guidance. His children grew up without a strong spiritual foundation because their father couldn't give what he didn't possess.

Emotionally, Marcus was unavailable and often harmful. He dismissed his wife's concerns as "emotional nonsense" and told his children to "toughen up" when they faced difficulties. He created an environment of emotional insecurity where family members learned to hide their feelings rather than share them.

When his eldest son began struggling with drug addiction, Marcus responded with anger and threats rather than love and guidance. When his daughter was sexually harassed at school, he dismissed her concerns and told her to "handle it herself." When his wife suffered from depression, he told her to "snap out of it" and threatened to leave if she didn't "get her act together."

Despite all his worldly qualifications as a protector, Marcus failed miserably in his God-given role. His family lived in fear rather than security, in emotional poverty despite material wealth, in spiritual darkness despite their church attendance. His protection was merely a facade that crumbled when his family faced real challenges.

A Faithful Example: The True Protector

In contrast, consider David, a man who understood and embodied the biblical role of protector. Physically, David was unremarkable—average height, slender build, and no formal training in combat or martial arts. Financially, he worked as a high school teacher and coach, earning a modest salary that required careful budgeting and occasional sacrifice.

Yet David was a true protector because he understood that his role flowed from his relationship with God rather than from his own strength or resources. He began each day with prayer and Scripture reading, seeking God's guidance for the challenges he would face. He prayed regularly for his wife and children, interceding for their needs and asking God to protect them from spiritual attack.

When his teenage son began questioning his faith, David didn't respond with arguments or threats but with patience and understanding. He spent hours listening to his son's doubts, answering his questions from Scripture, and sharing his own spiritual journey. He created a safe environment where his son could explore his faith without fear of rejection or condemnation.

When his daughter was being bullied at school, David didn't just tell her to "fight back" but taught her how to respond with wisdom and courage. He met with school officials, spoke with the bully's parents, and worked persistently until the situation was resolved. He protected his daughter not through aggression but through patient, persistent advocacy.

When his wife was diagnosed with a chronic illness, David became her primary caregiver without complaint. He researched her condition, found the best medical care available, and reorganized his schedule to accommodate her needs. He prayed for her healing while

71

accepting God's will for their lives, demonstrating faith that sustained the entire family.

Financially, David was creative and resourceful. When money was tight, he took on tutoring jobs and coaching clinics to provide for his family's needs. He taught his children the value of hard work and careful stewardship, involving them in family financial decisions and teaching them biblical principles of money management.

David's protection extended beyond his immediate family to his community. He mentored young men in his church, coached youth sports with emphasis on character development, and volunteered at a local crisis pregnancy center. He understood that his role as protector included protecting the vulnerable in his community.

When David faced his own spiritual battles, he sought help from mature believers and maintained accountability relationships with other godly men. He understood that he couldn't protect others if he wasn't protecting himself through spiritual disciplines and community support.

David's family experienced security not because of his wealth or physical strength but because of his consistent, loving leadership. His children grew up confident in their father's love and in God's faithfulness. His wife felt cherished and protected not because she was controlled but because she was valued and respected.

Protection as Worship

The Messianic Man's role as protector is fundamentally an act of worship. When he guards his family spiritually, physically, and emotionally, he is participating in God's own nature as protector and reflecting God's character to the world.

This worship dimension elevates protection from mere human obligation to sacred calling. The Messianic Man protects not simply because it's his duty but because it's his privilege to partner with God in caring for those He loves. Every act of protection becomes an offering of praise to the One who protects us all.

Protection as Imitation of God

"Therefore be imitators of God, as beloved children. And walk in love, just as Messiah also loved us and gave Himself up for us as an offering and sacrifice to God for a fragrant aroma" **(Ephesians 5:1-2, TLV)**. The Messianic Man protects because God protects, loves because God loves, and sacrifices because God sacrifices.

This divine imitation transforms the mundane aspects of protection into sacred acts. Changing the oil in his car becomes an act of worship when done to protect his family's safety. Working extra hours to pay for his daughter's education becomes an offering when done from love rather than obligation. Confronting his son's rebellious behavior becomes ministry when done with God's heart for restoration.

Protection as Stewardship

The Messianic Man understands that those under his care are not his possessions but God's gifts entrusted to his stewardship. He will give account to God for how he protected and cared for these precious souls. This accountability motivates him to excellence in protection and gives eternal significance to temporal acts of care.

Protection as Evangelism

The Messianic Man's faithful protection serves as a powerful testimony to the character of God. When unbelievers observe his sacrificial love, his consistent care, and his faithful provision, they see a reflection of God's love for humanity. His protection becomes a form of evangelism, drawing others to consider the God who inspires such devotion.

The Protector's Vigilance

The Hebrew word shamar implies constant vigilance, not just occasional attention. The Messianic Man develops a protective mindset that remains alert to threats and opportunities even during times of apparent peace.

Spiritual Vigilance

"Be sober and alert. Your adversary the devil prowls around like a roaring lion, seeking someone to devour" **(1 Peter 5:8, TLV)**. The Messianic Man maintains spiritual vigilance through regular prayer, Scripture study, and fellowship with other believers. He stays alert to spiritual attacks on his family, recognizing the enemy's tactics and responding with spiritual weapons.

This vigilance extends to monitoring the spiritual influences that affect his family—the media they consume, the friends they associate with, the ideas they encounter. He doesn't become paranoid or controlling but remains aware and engaged, ready to provide guidance and protection when needed.

Physical Vigilance

The Messianic Man pays attention to physical threats and safety concerns. He maintains situational awareness when out with his family, keeps his vehicle in good repair, and ensures his home is secure. He teaches his family basic safety principles and emergency procedures.

This vigilance also extends to health concerns, ensuring his family receives proper medical care, maintains good nutrition, and engages in appropriate physical activity. He doesn't live in fear but remains prudently aware of potential threats to his family's physical well-being.

Emotional Vigilance

The Messianic Man pays attention to the emotional climate of his home and family. He notices when family members are struggling emotionally and responds with appropriate care and support. He monitors his own emotional state, ensuring that his emotions don't become a source of threat to those he protects.

This emotional vigilance requires developing emotional intelligence and communication skills that may not come naturally to many men. He learns to read nonverbal cues, to listen actively, and to respond appropriately to emotional needs.

The Protector's Preparation

Effective protection requires preparation. The Messianic Man doesn't wait for threats to appear before preparing to meet them; he prepares himself spiritually, physically, and emotionally for the challenges he will face.

Spiritual Preparation
The Messianic Man prepares spiritually through regular disciplines of prayer, Scripture study, and fellowship. He develops his relationship with God not just for personal benefit but to be equipped for his role as protector. He studies Scripture to understand God's principles for protection and to develop the wisdom needed to apply those principles.

He also prepares through developing spiritual discernment, learning to recognize spiritual attacks and to respond with appropriate spiritual weapons. He memorizes Scripture that he can use in times of spiritual battle and develops the faith necessary to trust God in difficult circumstances.

Physical Preparation

The Messianic Man maintains his physical health and strength not from vanity but from love for those he protects. He keeps his body in condition to respond effectively to physical threats and to fulfill his responsibilities as provider and protector.

He may learn appropriate self-defense skills, not to become aggressive but to be prepared to protect his family if necessary. He develops practical skills that enable him to provide for his family's needs and to handle emergencies effectively.

He may even make decisions that will ultimately put his family in a better situation or out of harms way even when they don't see it.

Emotional Preparation

The Messianic Man prepares emotionally by developing emotional maturity and stability. He learns to manage his own emotions so they don't become a source of threat to his family. He develops communication skills that enable him to provide emotional support and guidance.

He also prepares by developing resilience, learning to handle stress and pressure without breaking down. He builds a support network of other godly men who can provide encouragement and accountability during difficult times.

The Protector's Wisdom

Protection requires wisdom to discern when to act and when to wait, when to be firm and when to be gentle, when to speak and when to remain silent. The Messianic Man seeks wisdom from God through prayer and Scripture study, understanding that human wisdom is insufficient for the challenges he faces.

Discerning Real Threats

The Messianic Man develops the ability to distinguish between real threats and false alarms. He doesn't become paranoid or overprotective but maintains appropriate vigilance. He learns to assess situations accurately and to respond proportionally to the actual level of threat.

Balancing Protection and Freedom

The Messianic Man must balance his protective instincts with the need to allow those under his care to grow and develop. He doesn't become overprotective to the point of stifling growth but provides appropriate boundaries and guidance while allowing appropriate freedom.

Choosing Appropriate Responses

The Messianic Man develops a range of responses to different threats, understanding that not every situation requires the same level of intervention. He learns when to respond with gentleness and when to respond with firmness, when to handle situations privately and when to involve others.

The Protector's Sacrifice

True protection often requires sacrifice. The Messianic Man must be willing to give up his own comfort, convenience, and even his life for the sake of those he protects. This sacrificial love reflects the heart of

God and demonstrates the depth of his commitment to his protective role.

Sacrificing Personal Desires

The Messianic Man regularly sacrifices his own desires for the benefit of those he protects. He may give up leisure activities to spend time with his family, forgo personal purchases to provide for their needs, or sacrifice career advancement to be available for them.

Sacrificing Comfort and Convenience

The Messianic Man accepts that his role as protector will often be inconvenient and uncomfortable. He may lose sleep caring for sick family members, work extra hours to provide for their needs, or endure discomfort to ensure their safety and well-being.

Sacrificing Life if Necessary

The ultimate sacrifice the Messianic Man must be prepared to make is his own life. Like Yeshua, who laid down His life for those He loved, the Messianic Man must be willing to give his life to protect those entrusted to his care.

The Protector's Dependence on God

Despite all his preparation and effort, the Messianic Man recognizes that his ability to protect is ultimately dependent on God's grace and power. He cannot protect effectively through his own strength but must rely on God's provision and guidance.

Trusting God's Sovereignty

The Messianic Man trusts that God is ultimately in control of all circumstances and that His purposes will be accomplished even when protection seems to fail. He does his best to fulfill his protective role while acknowledging that the outcome is in God's hands.

Seeking God's Guidance

The Messianic Man regularly seeks God's guidance in his protective role, asking for wisdom to know how to respond to different situations and for strength to fulfill his responsibilities. He recognizes that he needs divine guidance to protect effectively.

Relying on God's Power

The Messianic Man relies on God's power rather than his own strength to fulfill his protective role. He understands that spiritual battles require spiritual weapons and that physical protection often requires divine intervention.

The Protector and the Weaker Vessel

Scripture specifically addresses the man's responsibility to protect women as they are "the weaker vessel": *"Husbands, likewise, dwell with your wives with understanding, giving honor to the wife as to the weaker vessel, and as being heirs together of the grace of life, so that your prayers may not be hindered" (1 Peter 3:7, TLV).*

This designation of women as "the weaker vessel" is not a statement of inferiority but of difference. Just as a delicate crystal vase requires more careful handling than a sturdy clay pot, women often require different types of protection and care than men. The Messianic Man recognizes and honors these differences.

Physical Protection of Women

The Messianic Man understands that women are generally more vulnerable to physical threats and takes special care to protect them. He ensures their safety in potentially dangerous situations, accompanies them when necessary, and teaches them how to protect themselves when he cannot be present.

Emotional Protection of Women

The Messianic Man recognizes that women often process emotions differently than men and may be more vulnerable to emotional attack. He provides emotional stability and support, creating a safe environment where women can express their feelings without fear of judgment or rejection.

Spiritual Protection of Women

The Messianic Man takes special responsibility for the spiritual protection of women in his care, understanding that they may face unique spiritual challenges. He provides spiritual leadership and guidance while respecting their direct relationship with God.

The Protector and Children

Children hold a special place in God's heart, and the Messianic Man has a particular responsibility to protect them. Scripture clearly warns against harming children: *"You are not to mistreat any widow or orphan. If you mistreat them in any way, and they cry out to Me, I will surely hear their cry" (Exodus 22:22-23, TLV).*

Protecting Children from Physical Harm

The Messianic Man takes special care to protect children from physical harm, understanding that their size and inexperience make them particularly vulnerable. He creates safe environments for children to grow and develop while teaching them how to protect themselves.

Protecting Children from Emotional Harm

The Messianic Man protects children from emotional harm by creating stable, loving environments where they feel secure and valued. He speaks to children with kindness and respect, building their confidence and self-worth.

Protecting Children from Spiritual Harm

The Messianic Man has a special responsibility to protect children from spiritual harm, understanding that they are particularly vulnerable to spiritual deception and evil influence. He teaches them about God's love and protection while shielding them from harmful spiritual influences.

The Protector's Self-Defense

The Messianic Man cannot effectively protect others unless he first protects himself. This self-protection is not selfish but necessary for the fulfillment of his protective role.

Spiritual Self-Protection

The Messianic Man protects himself spiritually by maintaining his relationship with God through prayer, Scripture study, and fellowship. He puts on the full armor of God daily, preparing himself for spiritual battle.

"Finally, be strong in the Lord and in the strength of His might. Put on the whole armor of God, so that you may be able to stand against the schemes of the devil" (Ephesians 6:10-11, TLV). The Messianic Man understands that spiritual protection requires spiritual preparation and maintains his spiritual defenses through consistent studying of God's word, and being disciplined in it's application.

Physical Self-Protection

The Messianic Man maintains his physical health and strength not from vanity but from love for those he protects. He keeps his body in condition to fulfill his responsibilities and to respond effectively to physical threats.

Emotional Self-Protection
The Messianic Man protects himself emotionally by maintaining healthy relationships and boundaries. He seeks support from other godly men and doesn't try to carry all burdens alone.

Intellectual Self-Protection
The Messianic Man protects his mind by being careful about what he reads, watches, and thinks about. He follows Paul's instruction: *"Finally, brothers, whatever is true, whatever is honorable, whatever is right, whatever is pure, whatever is lovely, whatever is admirable—if anything is excellent or praiseworthy—think on these things" (Philippians 4:8, TLV).*

The Protector's Legacy
The Messianic Man's role as protector extends beyond his immediate family to future generations. The protection he provides today creates a legacy that will impact his children's children and the generations that follow.

Teaching the Next Generation
The Messianic Man teaches his children how to be protectors themselves, passing on the wisdom and skills they will need to fulfill their own protective roles. He models protective behavior and explains the biblical principles that guide his actions.

Creating Generational Blessing

The Messianic Man's faithful protection creates a legacy of blessing that extends to future generations. His children learn to trust God's protection because they experienced their father's faithful care. They learn to protect others because they were protected themselves.

Building Strong Families

The Messianic Man's protection strengthens his family unit, creating a foundation of love and security that can withstand the challenges of life. This strong foundation enables his family to weather storms and to provide stability for future generations.

The Protector's Calling

The role of protector is not merely a cultural expectation or personal preference but a divine calling. The Messianic Man who embraces this calling joins a long line of faithful men who have protected God's people throughout history.

From Abraham, who protected his household and rescued his nephew, to David, who protected Israel from its enemies, to the apostles, who protected the early church from false teaching, godly men have always understood their calling to protect others.

The Messianic Man who fulfills his role as protector participates in God's own nature as protector and reflects God's character to the world. He becomes a living testimony to God's love and faithfulness, demonstrating through his actions the reality of divine protection.

This calling requires sacrifice, commitment, and dependence on God's grace. It is not easy, but it is essential. The Messianic Man who embraces this calling will find that his life gains meaning and purpose as he participates in God's work of protection and redemption.

The world desperately needs men who understand and fulfill their God-given role as protectors. In an age of confusion about masculine identity and purpose, the Messianic Man who stands firm in his calling provides a beacon of hope and stability. He demonstrates that true strength comes from God, that real protection flows from love, and that authentic masculinity is defined by service rather than dominance.

As the Messianic Man fulfills his role as protector, he discovers that in protecting others, he himself is protected by the ultimate Protector. In serving others, he serves God. In laying down his life for others, he finds life. This is the paradox of biblical protection: in giving up everything for others, the protector gains everything that truly matters.

The Weight and Wound of Protection

Every act of true protection carries within it the echo of the Cross—the paradox of strength in surrender, power in sacrifice. The Messianic Man does not guard his own life, for he has already laid it down. His protection is not an assertion of control, but a relinquishing of it. He stands as a sentinel in the night, not because he fears the darkness, but because he knows the Light that will inevitably break it.

Yet this role is not without its wounds. To protect is to make oneself a shield—to absorb the blows meant for others. The Messianic Man bears the scars of intercession, the exhaustion of vigilance, the loneliness of leadership. He is often misunderstood, for the world cannot comprehend a strength that does not dominate, an authority that does not oppress. He is accused of being too harsh when he sets boundaries, too soft when he shows mercy. The serpent whispers that he is failing, that his sacrifices are in vain, that his strength is insufficient.

But the Messianic Man knows a deeper truth: his protection is not his own. It is an extension of the One who *"will not let your foot slip—your Guardian will not slumber"* **(Psalm 121:3, TLV)**. His weariness is met with divine strength; his inadequacy is swallowed by God's sufficiency.

The Protector's Lament

There are nights when the Messianic Man kneels in the silence of his own Gethsemane, sweat like blood upon his brow, wrestling with the weight of his calling. *Abba, Father! All things are possible for You! Take this cup from me!" (Mark 14:36, TLV)*. He feels the crushing responsibility—the fear that he will fail, that his loved ones will suffer because of his shortcomings.

But in that moment of raw honesty, he hears the whisper of the Spirit:

"You are not their savior. I AM."

The Messianic Man is not Messiah. He is a vessel, a conduit, a shadow of the True Protector. His role is not to bear the world's burdens alone, but to point those he guards to the One who *"daily bears our burdens" (Psalm 68:19, TLV)*.

The Protector's Reward

The world does not applaud the quiet victories of the Messianic Man. There are no medals for the nights he spends in prayer, no trophies for the tears he sheds in intercession, no headlines for the daily deaths to self that true protection requires.

But there is a reward—one that the flesh cannot see, but the spirit knows. It is the joy of seeing his wife flourish in security, his children walk in truth, his spiritual sons rise up as warriors of light. It is the quiet affirmation of the Father: *"Well done, good and faithful servant" (Matthew 25:21, TLV)*. It is the legacy of a life poured out—an offering that does not return void.

Final Exhortation: The Protector's Charge

Messianic Man, hear your calling:

You are a guardian of souls.
A keeper of the flame.
A watchman on the wall.

You will be misunderstood.
You will be weary.
You will sometimes stand alone.

But you are not forgotten.
You are not forsaken.
You are not powerless.

The God who commands you is the God who equips you.
The One who calls you is the One who sustains you.

So rise.
Stand firm.
Hold fast.

The night is dark, but the dawn is sure.

SYNOPSIS: THE MESSIANIC MAN AS PROTECTOR

In a world that glorifies counterfeit strength—brute force, financial dominance, and performative heroism—the Messianic Man is called to a higher, holier standard of protection. He is not a tyrant, nor a passive observer, but a living embodiment of chesed (covenant love) and gevurah (holy strength).

1. **The World's Counterfeit** – Society mistakes domination for protection, wealth for provision, and aggression for

leadership. But the Messianic Man knows true protection is rooted in surrender to God, not reliance on self.

2. **The Biblical Mandate** – From shamar (to guard) in Genesis to the armor of God in Ephesians, Scripture frames protection as spiritual before it is physical. The Messianic Man's first duty is intercession, his first weapon the Word.

3. **The Dimensions of Protection**

- **Spiritual** – He wages war in prayer, teaches truth, and models righteousness.
- **Physical** – He defends, provides, and creates safety without idolizing strength.
- **Emotional** – He is a safe harbor, speaking life, not death, into fragile hearts.

4. **The Ultimate Model: Yeshua** – Messiah's life was one of fierce protection—healing the broken, confronting demons, and ultimately laying down His life. The Messianic Man follows in His steps.

5. **The Cost** – Protection requires sacrifice—time, comfort, pride, sometimes even reputation. The Messianic Man bleeds so others don't have to.

6. **The Paradox** – In losing his life for others, he finds it. In surrendering control, he gains divine authority. In becoming weak, he taps into God's strength.

7. **The Legacy** – His protection echoes into eternity. Generations will rise and call him blessed, not because he was perfect, but because he pointed them to the Perfect Protector.

Final Truth:

The Messianic Man's protection is not about him at all. It is about reflecting the One who neither slumbers nor sleeps. It is about magnifying the Lion of Judah who became the Lamb slain. It is about proclaiming, in word and deed:

"The Lord is my rock, my fortress, and my deliverer. My God is my rock, in whom I take refuge, my shield, and the horn of my salvation. My stronghold." **(Psalm 18:2, TLV).**

"No murder is so sweet to me as the slow ruin of the Messianic Man. The Messianic Man is the sacrificial lamb appointed by God—silence him, and the altar of the family runs red." — The Adversary

So guard well, Messianic Man.

The night is fading.

The Morning Star is rising.

CHAPTER FOUR: THE MESSIANIC LEADER – A DIVINE CALL TO SERVANT LEADERSHIP

The World's Distorted View of Leadership

Contemporary society has constructed a fundamentally flawed paradigm of leadership, one that elevates superficial qualities while ignoring the deeper character traits that define true authority. This worldly perspective, orchestrated by the Adversary's deceptive influence, prioritizes external charisma over internal integrity, public appeal over private virtue, and personal ambition over sacrificial service.

Modern leadership selection often hinges on charismatic presence—the ability to captivate audiences through eloquent speech and magnetic personality. This emphasis on performative leadership creates a dangerous precedent where style supersedes substance. We witness this phenomenon repeatedly in political arenas, where candidates are chosen based on their ability to deliver compelling rhetoric rather than their moral foundation or spiritual maturity. The result is a leadership class that excels at public relations but fails at righteous governance.

The secular world also equates leadership with raw power and dominance. This paradigm suggests that effective leaders must possess the ability to control others through force, intimidation, or manipulation. However, this understanding fundamentally misrepresents authentic authority. True strength is not demonstrated through the subjugation of others but through the willing sacrifice of oneself for those under one's care. History repeatedly demonstrates that the most physically imposing individuals are often guided by those who possess superior wisdom and strategic thinking, revealing the hollow nature of leadership based solely on physical dominance.

Democratic systems and corporate environments frequently elevate individuals based on popularity contests rather than competence evaluations. This approach mirrors the high school dynamics where the "popular kid" receives positions of responsibility not because of qualifications but due to social appeal. Such selection processes inevitably place unqualified individuals in positions of tremendous responsibility, creating systemic failures that impact countless lives.

Additionally, society persistently associates leadership with material success, assuming that wealth accumulation or professional achievement automatically qualifies someone for positions of authority. This materialistic perspective ignores the reality that worldly success often comes at the expense of moral integrity and spiritual development. The pursuit of financial gain can corrupt even well-intentioned individuals, making them unsuitable for leading others toward righteousness.

These superficial criteria consistently produce leaders who lack moral grounding, spiritual maturity, and genuine concern for those they govern. Instead of seeking wisdom, compassion, and integrity, society's emphasis on external factors results in leadership that prioritizes personal advancement over collective spiritual well-being.

God's Blueprint for Leadership

From the Almighty's perspective, leadership represents a sacred calling rooted in servanthood, humility, and unwavering obedience to divine will. Biblical leadership principles stand in stark contrast to worldly standards, emphasizing heart transformation over external presentation and character development over charismatic appeal.

The Hebrew language provides profound insights into divine leadership concepts. The term "nagid" signifies a prince or leader who has been divinely appointed, while "rosh" denotes the head or chief who provides direction and guidance. In Greek, "archon" describes a ruler who governs with authority, and "hegemon" refers to a guide or commander who leads others forward. These linguistic foundations reveal that authentic leadership involves guidance, direction, and the responsibility to shepherd others according to divine principles.

The concept of servant leadership, embodied in the Hebrew word "eved", forms the cornerstone of biblical authority. This principle finds its ultimate expression in Moses, who reluctantly accepted leadership not from personal ambition but from obedience to God's calling (Exodus 3:10-12). Moses exemplified the paradox of godly leadership: the most qualified leaders are often those who least desire the position, recognizing the weight of responsibility it carries.

Yeshua the Messiah reinforced this servant leadership model when He declared, "Whoever wants to become great among you must be your servant, and whoever wants to be first must be slave of all" (Mark 10:43-44). This revolutionary statement challenges every worldly assumption about leadership, establishing that true greatness emerges through self-sacrifice rather than self-promotion.

The shepherd metaphor, represented by the Hebrew word "ro'eh", provides another essential framework for understanding godly leadership. A shepherd leads with careful attention to the needs of his flock, providing protection, guidance, and nourishment. King David embodied this principle both literally as a young shepherd and figuratively as Israel's king, leading "with integrity of heart and skillful hands" (Psalm 78:72). The shepherd-leader recognizes that his primary responsibility is the welfare of those entrusted to his care, not his own comfort or advancement.

Humility, expressed through the Hebrew concept of "anavah", represents an indispensable quality of godly leadership. Moses was described as "very humble, more than anyone else on the face of the earth" (Numbers 12:3), enabling him to rely completely on divine guidance rather than human wisdom. Humble leaders understand that their authority originates from God alone and that they will be held accountable for their stewardship of that authority.

This divine appointment principle applies across all levels of leadership, from national governments to household authority. Whether in democratic, monarchical, or authoritarian systems, God sovereignly orchestrates the placement of leaders according to His purposes. As stated in Romans 13:1, "Everyone must submit himself to the governing authorities, for there is no authority except that which God has established." This truth encompasses presidents, governors, mayors, corporate executives, and heads of households, all of whom serve under divine appointment and accountability.

The military model provides an excellent illustration of proper leadership hierarchy. Each rank maintains respect for the chain of command, with subordinates honoring their superiors while superiors remain accountable to their commanding officers. This structure ensures order, discipline, and effective mission accomplishment. Similarly, godly leaders must maintain submission to their divine Commander while exercising responsible authority over those in their care.

A leader from God's perspective must operate with righteousness, ensuring justice and fairness in all decisions while upholding divine law (Proverbs 29:2). This commitment to righteousness extends beyond mere rule-following to encompass a heart transformation that naturally produces just and compassionate decisions. Leaders are called to reflect God's character in their interactions with others, particularly in their treatment of the vulnerable and marginalized.

Obedience, captured in the Hebrew word "shema", meaning "to hear" or "to listen," underscores the essential nature of godly leadership. Leaders like Joshua achieved success because they meditated on God's Word day and night, allowing divine wisdom to guide their decisions (Joshua 1:8). This continuous engagement with

Scripture enables leaders to discern God's will and respond appropriately to challenging circumstances.

True godly leadership empowers others rather than hoarding authority. This principle is demonstrated in Exodus 18:13-27, where Jethro advises Moses to delegate responsibilities to capable men, distributing the leadership burden and developing other leaders. Effective leaders multiply themselves by investing in the development of others, creating sustainable leadership structures that outlast their own tenure.

At its foundation, godly leadership flows from love—a deep, sacrificial commitment to seeking the well-being of those under one's care. This aligns with Yeshua's teaching about loving one another as He loved us (John 13:34), a love that extends to the point of self-sacrifice for others' benefit.

The Messianic Man as an Integral Leader

The Messianic Man must embody integrity in every aspect of his leadership role, understanding that his character forms the foundation upon which all other leadership qualities are built. Integrity, derived from the Latin "integer" meaning whole or complete, represents the alignment of one's inner beliefs with outward actions. For the Messianic Man, this means living according to biblical principles regardless of external pressures or personal cost.

Understanding Integral Leadership

Integral leadership requires the Messianic Man to be whole, complete, and undivided in his commitment to righteousness. This wholeness manifests in several key areas:

Spiritual Integrity: The Messianic Man maintains consistency between his private devotional life and public leadership. He cannot compartmentalize his faith, relegating it to Sunday morning worship while operating according to worldly principles throughout the week. His relationship with God must permeate every decision, conversation, and action.

Moral Integrity: His ethical standards remain unwavering regardless of circumstances. Whether facing financial pressure, social expectations, or personal desires, the Messianic Man adheres to biblical morality. He understands that compromise in small matters leads to corruption in larger ones, and he therefore maintains vigilance over his character.

Relational Integrity: He treats all people with dignity and respect, regardless of their position, wealth, or social status. His interactions with subordinates reflect the same kindness he shows to superiors, demonstrating that his character is not situational but consistent.

Intellectual Integrity: The Messianic Man commits to truth, even when it proves inconvenient or unpopular. He refuses to manipulate information for personal advantage and acknowledges his limitations rather than pretending to possess knowledge he lacks.

Leading Men Toward Righteousness

The Messianic Man bears the sacred responsibility of guiding other men, particularly younger men, toward biblical masculinity and righteous living. This mentorship role extends beyond formal teaching to include modeling appropriate behavior and creating accountability relationships.

Modeling Respectful Behavior: Young men learn respect primarily through observation rather than instruction. The Messianic Man demonstrates respect in his interactions with authority figures, his treatment of women, and his engagement with peers. He shows that respect is not weakness but strength under control.

Teaching Honesty: In a culture that often rewards deception and manipulation, the Messianic Man must actively teach and model honesty. He demonstrates that truthfulness, even when costly. He builds trust and character. He helps younger men understand that integrity is more valuable than temporary advantage gained through dishonesty.

Developing Trustworthiness: The Messianic Man proves himself trustworthy through consistent behavior over time. He keeps his commitments, maintains confidentiality when appropriate, and follows through on his promises. By demonstrating reliability, he teaches other men the importance of being men of their word.

Cultivating Caring Hearts: Contrary to cultural stereotypes about masculine stoicism, the Messianic Man models appropriate emotional expression and genuine care for others. He shows that true strength includes the ability to empathize with others' struggles and respond with compassion.

Establishing Accountability: The Messianic Man creates structures for mutual accountability among men, understanding that isolation leads to moral compromise. He participates in authentic relationships where men can confess struggles, seek guidance, and receive support in their spiritual growth.

Leading Women with Wisdom and Honor

The Messianic Man's leadership of women requires particular wisdom, recognizing both the unique strengths that women bring and the biblical principles that govern gender relationships. This leadership must be characterized by honor, protection, and servant-hearted guidance.

Protective Leadership: The Messianic Man understands his responsibility to protect women from physical, emotional, and spiritual harm. This protection extends beyond his immediate family to encompass all women within his sphere of influence. He uses his position and resources to create safe environments where women can flourish.

Honoring Feminine Strengths: Rather than viewing women as inferior or merely instrumental, the Messianic Man recognizes and celebrates the unique gifts that women contribute to family, church, and society. He seeks to understand and appreciate feminine perspectives, recognizing that they often provide insights that complement masculine viewpoints.

Serving Through Leadership: His leadership of women follows the Messianic model of servant leadership, where authority is exercised for the benefit of those being led rather than for personal advantage. He makes decisions that prioritize women's spiritual, emotional, and physical well-being over his own convenience.

Teaching and Mentoring: The Messianic Man serves as a teacher and mentor to women, particularly in areas where biblical principles provide guidance. This teaching role must be exercised with humility, recognizing that he too is a learner in the school of divine wisdom.

Educational Leadership Responsibilities

The Messianic Man bears particular responsibility for the education and spiritual development of young people, including both young men and women. This educational leadership encompasses several key areas:

Spiritual Formation: He takes active responsibility for teaching biblical principles, not merely delegating this task to professional clergy or educational institutions. He creates regular opportunities for spiritual instruction, discussion, and application.

Character Development: Beyond academic instruction, the Messianic Man prioritizes character formation, helping young people develop integrity, wisdom, and moral courage. He understands that character formation occurs primarily through relationship and example rather than formal instruction.

Practical Life Skills: He ensures that young people under his influence develop practical skills necessary for adult life, including financial management, interpersonal communication, and problem-solving abilities.

Cultural Engagement: The Messianic Man helps young people understand how to engage thoughtfully with contemporary culture while maintaining biblical convictions. He teaches discernment rather than mere separation, equipping them to be "in the world but not of the world."

Three Dimensions of Messianic Leadership

Spiritual Leadership: The Foundation of Authority

Spiritual leadership forms the cornerstone of all authentic authority, as it addresses the fundamental question of ultimate allegiance. The Messianic Man must establish his relationship with God as the primary source of his leadership authority, recognizing that all earthly authority flows from divine appointment.

The essence of spiritual leadership involves creating and maintaining an environment where spiritual growth can flourish. This requires the leader to model authentic spiritual life through consistent prayer, Scripture study, and worship. The Messianic Man cannot compartmentalize his spirituality, treating it as a private matter separate from his leadership responsibilities. Instead, his spiritual life must permeate every aspect of his leadership, providing the foundation for all decisions and actions.

Yeshua the Messiah exemplified this principle through His consistent pattern of withdrawing for prayer and communion with the Father *(Luke 5:16)*. Despite the pressing demands of ministry and the needs of those around Him, He prioritized His relationship with God, understanding that this relationship provided the source of His authority and wisdom. Similarly, the Messianic Man must establish regular patterns of spiritual discipline that maintain his connection to divine guidance.

Spiritual leadership also involves teaching others to develop their own relationship with God. The Messianic Man serves as a spiritual mentor, helping others understand biblical principles and apply them to their daily lives. This teaching role requires both knowledge of Scripture and the ability to communicate spiritual truths in ways that others can understand and apply.

In practical terms, spiritual leadership might involve leading family devotions, facilitating Bible study groups, or simply engaging in conversations that point others toward spiritual truth. The key is consistency and authenticity—the Messianic Man must demonstrate that his spiritual convictions are genuine and that they produce tangible benefits in his life and the lives of those he leads.

Emotional Leadership: Stability in the Storm

Emotional leadership requires the Messianic Man to demonstrate emotional maturity, stability, and wisdom in his interactions with others. This dimension of leadership is particularly crucial during times of crisis, conflict, or uncertainty, when those under his care look to him for stability and direction.

The foundation of emotional leadership is the *"peace that surpasses understanding"* **(Philippians 4:7)**, which enables the leader to remain calm and focused during turbulent circumstances. This supernatural peace comes from deep trust in God's sovereignty and goodness, allowing the leader to face challenges with confidence rather than anxiety.

Emotional leadership also involves the ability to understand and respond appropriately to the emotional needs of others. The Messianic Man must develop empathy and compassion, recognizing that those under his care experience various emotional struggles and need guidance and support. This requires active listening, patience, and the wisdom to know when to offer advice and when to simply provide comfort.

Joseph's life provides an excellent example of emotional leadership. Despite experiencing betrayal by his brothers, false accusation by Potiphar's wife, and abandonment by fellow prisoners, Joseph maintained emotional stability and eventually demonstrated extraordinary forgiveness and wisdom. When reunited with his brothers, he chose reconciliation over revenge, providing for their needs during a time of famine *(Genesis 45:4-8)*. His emotional maturity enabled him to see God's sovereign purpose in his suffering and to respond with grace rather than bitterness.

The Messianic Man must also demonstrate emotional leadership within his household, particularly in managing family finances and making difficult decisions. During times of financial stress or uncertainty, family members look to him for stability and confidence. His emotional response to these challenges sets the tone for the entire household's response. If he demonstrates anxiety and despair, others will follow suit. If he maintains peace and trust in God's provision, he creates an environment where others can rest secure despite external circumstances.

Physical Leadership: Provision and Protection

Physical leadership involves the tangible responsibilities of providing for and protecting those under one's care. This dimension of leadership requires practical skills, hard work, and strategic thinking to ensure that the basic needs of dependents are met and that they are protected from harm.

The provision aspect of physical leadership extends beyond mere financial support to encompass the creation of stable, nurturing environments where others can flourish. This includes ensuring adequate food, shelter, clothing, and healthcare, but it also involves creating emotional and spiritual safety where individuals can develop their potential without fear of harm or neglect.

Nehemiah exemplified physical leadership during the rebuilding of Jerusalem's walls. Faced with both external opposition and internal challenges, he demonstrated remarkable organizational skills, strategic thinking, and personal courage. He organized the workers efficiently, provided for their protection against enemy attacks, and maintained morale throughout the difficult project *(Nehemiah 4:13-23)*. His physical leadership ensured not only the completion of the construction project but also the security and encouragement of the workers.

The protection aspect of physical leadership requires the Messianic Man to be vigilant concerning threats to those under his care. This vigilance extends beyond physical dangers to include spiritual and emotional threats. He must be aware of harmful influences that might impact his family or community and take appropriate action to address these threats.

Physical leadership also involves modeling hard work and stewardship. The Messianic Man demonstrates through his own example that productive work is honorable and necessary. He teaches others the value of diligence, persistence, and excellence in their endeavors, showing that physical labor and practical skills are important components of a well-rounded life which ultimately points to God.

Exemplars of Leadership: Contrasting Models

King David: A Heart After God Despite Human Frailty

King David stands as perhaps the most compelling example of godly leadership in Scripture, not because of his perfection but because of his genuine heart for God despite significant personal failures. His designation as *"a man after God's own heart" (1 Samuel 13:14; Acts 13:22)* stems not from moral perfection but from his consistent desire to align his life with God's will and his genuine repentance when he fell short.

David's Spiritual Leadership: Throughout his life, David maintained a vibrant relationship with God that permeated his leadership. His psalms reveal a man who regularly poured out his heart to God in both praise and petition. As king, he prioritized the restoration of proper worship in Israel, bringing the Ark of the Covenant to Jerusalem and establishing organized worship practices *(2 Samuel 6)*. His spiritual leadership created an environment where the worship of God flourished throughout the kingdom.

David's spiritual authenticity is particularly evident in his response to his moral failure with Bathsheba. Rather than attempting to cover up his sin or justify his actions, he accepted Nathan's rebuke and composed *Psalm 51*, one of the most profound expressions of repentance in Scripture. This response demonstrates that godly leaders acknowledge their failures and seek genuine restoration rather than merely managing their public image.

David's Emotional Leadership: David demonstrated remarkable emotional intelligence and maturity in his relationships with others. His friendship with Jonathan, his treatment of Saul despite Saul's attempts to kill him, and his grieving for his enemies revealed a man capable of deep emotional connection and genuine compassion. Even in his relationship with his rebellious son Absalom, David's emotional response demonstrated the heart of a father who loved his son despite his son's betrayal.

David's emotional leadership is perhaps most clearly seen in his response to Saul's persecution. Despite having multiple opportunities to kill Saul and claim the throne, David refused to harm *"the Lord's anointed" (1 Samuel 24:6)*. His emotional restraint and respect for God's appointed authority revealed a leader who could subordinate his personal desires to higher principles.

David's Physical Leadership: As a military leader, David demonstrated exceptional courage and strategic thinking. His victory over Goliath as a young man established his reputation as a warrior who trusted in God's power rather than conventional military might

(1 Samuel 17). As king, he led Israel's armies to numerous victories, establishing Israel as a dominant regional power.

David's physical leadership extended beyond military prowess to encompass administrative and organizational skills. He established effective governmental structures, expanded Israel's territory, and created the economic and political foundation for Solomon's later achievements. His leadership transformed Israel from a loose confederation of tribes into a unified, prosperous kingdom.

King Saul: The Tragic Failure of Self-Centered Leadership

King Saul serves as a cautionary example of how leadership can be corrupted by pride, disobedience, and self-centeredness. His failure demonstrates the devastating consequences when leaders prioritize their own interests over their responsibility to God and those they serve.

Saul's Spiritual Failure: Saul's spiritual decline began with his unwillingness to wait for God's timing and his assumption of priestly duties that were not his responsibility *(1 Samuel 13:8-14)*. This act of presumption revealed a leader who was more concerned with maintaining his position and public image than with obeying God's commands. His later disobedience in sparing King Agag and the best of the Amalekite livestock *(1 Samuel 15:9-23)* demonstrated that he valued human approval over divine approval.

Saul's spiritual failure culminated in his consultation with the witch of Endor *(1 Samuel 28)*, an act that directly violated God's commands regarding occult practices. This desperate act revealed a leader who had lost his connection to God and was willing to seek guidance from forbidden sources rather than repent and seek restoration.

Saul's Emotional Failure: Saul's emotional instability became increasingly apparent as his reign progressed. His jealousy of David's success and popularity consumed him, leading to irrational and destructive behavior. Rather than celebrating David's victories as beneficial to Israel, Saul perceived them as threats to his own position and sought to eliminate David *(1 Samuel 18:7-9)*.

This jealousy created a toxic environment within the royal court and divided the nation. Saul's inability to control his emotions and his tendency to make decisions based on personal insecurity rather than national interest demonstrate the importance of emotional maturity in leadership.

Saul's Physical Failure: Saul's physical leadership deteriorated as he became increasingly focused on personal vendettas rather than national defense. His pursuit of David consumed resources and attention that should have been directed toward protecting Israel from external threats. His failure to unite the nation and his creation of internal conflict weakened Israel's ability to respond effectively to enemy attacks.

The contrast between Saul's early promise and his eventual failure illustrates how leadership can be corrupted when personal interests supersede service to God and others. His trajectory serves as a warning to all leaders about the dangers of pride, disobedience, and self-centeredness.

Contemporary Applications of Messianic Leadership

Judicial Leadership: Righteousness in the Courtroom

Judges occupy a unique position in society, wielding significant authority over the lives and liberties of citizens. The Messianic Man serving in judicial capacity must understand that his courtroom represents a sacred space where God's justice is to be administered through human instruments.

Spiritual Dimension: The godly judge recognizes that ultimate justice belongs to God and that his role is to serve as an instrument of divine justice. He begins each day with prayer, seeking wisdom and discernment for the decisions he must make. He understands that his authority comes from God and that he will be held accountable for how he exercises that authority. He ensures that God's principles of justice, mercy, and truth guide his decisions rather than political expediency or personal preference.

Emotional Dimension: The righteous judge maintains emotional equilibrium while demonstrating appropriate compassion for those who appear before him. He carefully considers the hearts and motivations of both victims and defendants, seeking to understand the full context of each situation. He avoids favoritism based on wealth, social status, or personal relationships, treating all individuals with equal dignity and respect.

Physical Dimension: The judge's courtroom presence reflects the dignity and authority of his position. He maintains order and decorum while creating an atmosphere where truth can be established and justice can be served. He ensures that all parties receive fair treatment and that the proceedings are conducted with integrity and transparency.

Executive Leadership: Governing with Divine Wisdom

Presidents and other executive leaders bear tremendous responsibility for the welfare of their citizens. The Messianic Man in executive position must understand that his authority comes from God and that he serves as a steward of the people's trust.

Spiritual Dimension: The godly executive leader promotes policies and initiatives that align with biblical principles of justice, compassion, and righteousness. He seeks to create an environment where citizens can worship God freely and live according to their convictions. He understands that a nation's prosperity depends ultimately on its relationship with God and he seeks to lead in ways that honor divine principles.

Emotional Dimension: The wise executive leader demonstrates empathy and understanding for the struggles of his citizens, particularly those who are marginalized or disadvantaged. He maintains emotional stability during crises, providing reassurance and direction when others are fearful or uncertain. He makes decisions based on principle rather than popular opinion, understanding that true leadership sometimes requires making unpopular choices for the long-term benefit of the nation.

Physical Dimension: The executive leader demonstrates his commitment to his people through his physical presence and active engagement with their concerns. He visits disaster areas, meets with citizens, and maintains visibility to demonstrate his care and concern. He makes difficult decisions regarding national security and defense, understanding that his choices have life-and-death implications for those he serves.

Corporate Leadership: Stewarding Resources for Kingdom Purposes

CEOs and other corporate leaders manage significant resources and influence the lives of numerous employees and stakeholders. The Messianic Man in corporate leadership must understand that his business serves a higher purpose than mere profit generation.

Spiritual Dimension: The godly CEO recognizes that his business belongs ultimately to God and that he serves as a steward of the resources entrusted to him. He seeks to operate according to biblical principles of integrity, fairness, and stewardship. He views his employees as image-bearers of God deserving of dignity and respect, not merely as resources to be exploited for profit.

Emotional Dimension: The wise corporate leader creates a work environment where employees feel valued, respected, and empowered to contribute their best efforts. He demonstrates genuine care for their well-being and development, understanding that businesses thrive when people flourish. He maintains emotional stability during challenging business conditions, providing steady leadership when others are anxious about their security.

Physical Dimension: The corporate leader demonstrates his commitment to his organization through active engagement with employees at all levels. He maintains visibility throughout the organization, understanding the challenges and opportunities that exist at different levels. He makes strategic decisions that balance the needs of various stakeholders while maintaining the long-term health of the organization.

Legal Advocacy: Pursuing Justice and Truth

Lawyers serve as advocates within the legal system, representing clients and seeking justice through legal processes. The Messianic Man practicing law must understand that his profession provides an opportunity to serve others and pursue justice according to biblical principles.

Spiritual Dimension: The godly lawyer recognizes that his ultimate loyalty belongs to God and that he must practice law according to divine principles of truth and justice. He refuses to participate in deceptive practices or to manipulate the legal system for personal advantage. He provides equal representation to all clients regardless of their ability to pay, understanding that access to justice is a fundamental human right.

Emotional Dimension: The wise lawyer demonstrates empathy and compassion for clients who are experiencing legal difficulties. He provides honest counsel even when it may disappoint clients, understanding that truth serves their long-term interests better than false hope. He maintains emotional equilibrium during challenging cases, providing steady guidance when clients are anxious or distraught.

Physical Dimension: The lawyer demonstrates his commitment to his clients through diligent preparation and vigorous advocacy. He maintains high professional standards and treats all participants in the legal process with respect and dignity. He uses his knowledge and skills to serve the cause of justice rather than merely to advance his own career.

Paternal Leadership: Raising the Next Generation

Fathers bear the sacred responsibility of raising children who will contribute positively to society and live according to divine principles. The Messianic Man as father must understand that his role extends far beyond financial provision to encompass spiritual, emotional, and moral development.

Spiritual Dimension: The godly father serves as the spiritual leader of his household, creating an environment where faith can flourish and where children learn to know and love God. He leads family devotions, teaches biblical principles, and demonstrates through his own life what it means to follow God faithfully. He prays regularly for his children and seeks divine wisdom in his parenting decisions.

Emotional Dimension: The wise father creates emotional safety for his children, providing a secure environment where they can develop their personalities and gifts without fear of rejection or abandonment. He demonstrates appropriate emotional expression and teaches his children how to process their own emotions in healthy ways. He listens actively to his children's concerns and provides guidance that helps them navigate the challenges of growing up.

Physical Dimension: The father demonstrates his love for his children through active involvement in their lives. He participates in their activities, helps with their education, and ensures that their physical needs are met. He teaches practical skills and work ethic, preparing them for adult responsibilities. He protects them from harm while allowing them appropriate freedom to learn and grow.

Marital Leadership: Serving Through Headship

Husbands bear the responsibility of loving leadership within marriage, serving their wives according to the biblical model of Messiah's love for the church. The Messianic Man as husband must understand that his headship is expressed through sacrificial service rather than authoritarian control.

Spiritual Dimension: The godly husband serves as the spiritual leader of his marriage, initiating spiritual activities and creating an environment where his wife can grow in her relationship with God. He leads by example, demonstrating what it means to follow the Messiah faithfully. He prays for his wife and seeks divine wisdom in his role as husband.

Emotional Dimension: The wise husband demonstrates emotional intelligence and maturity in his relationship with his wife. He listens actively to her concerns, validates her emotions, and provides emotional support during challenging times. He celebrates her successes and provides encouragement during difficulties. He creates emotional intimacy through vulnerable communication and consistent care.

Physical Dimension: The husband demonstrates his love through acts of service and provision. He works diligently to provide for his family's needs and creates a safe, comfortable home environment. He serves his wife through practical assistance and thoughtful gestures that demonstrate his care and commitment.

Conclusion: The Call to Messianic Leadership

True leadership, as ordained by the Almighty, transcends the shallow metrics of worldly success and power. The Messianic Man is called to a higher standard—one that reflects the character of Yeshua the Messiah, who demonstrated that authentic authority flows from sacrificial love, humble service, and unwavering obedience to the Father's will.

The world desperately needs leaders who understand that their authority comes not from human appointment but from divine calling, that their purpose is not self-advancement but service to others, and that their legacy will be measured not by earthly achievements but by their faithfulness to God's standards. The Messianic Man must embrace this calling with both humility and courage, recognizing that leadership is not a privilege to be enjoyed but a responsibility to be stewarded.

Like David, the Messianic Man may face personal failures and moral struggles, but his heart remains oriented toward God, quick to repent when he falls short and committed to growing in spiritual maturity. Unlike Saul, he refuses to allow pride, jealousy, or self-interest to corrupt his leadership, instead maintaining his focus on serving God and others faithfully.

The three dimensions of leadership—spiritual, emotional, and physical—must work in harmony within the Messianic Man's life. His spiritual leadership provides the foundation for all other aspects of his authority, ensuring that his decisions align with divine principles. His emotional leadership creates an environment where others can flourish, providing stability and wisdom during challenging times. His physical leadership translates his spiritual and emotional commitments into tangible actions that benefit those under his care.

Whether serving as a judge, executive, corporate leader, attorney, father, or husband, the Messianic Man must remember that his ultimate accountability is to God, who appointed him to his position and who will evaluate his stewardship when he stands before the Messiah. This accountability should both humble him and empower him, knowing that his authority comes from the highest source and that his service contributes to the advancing of God's kingdom on earth.

The call to Messianic leadership is not easy, but it is essential. The world needs men who will stand for truth when it is unpopular, who will serve others when it is costly, and who will lead with integrity when it is inconvenient. The Messianic Man must answer this call, not for personal glory but for the sake of those entrusted to his care and for the honor of the One who called him to serve.

As Yeshua declared, *"Whoever wants to be first must be last of all and servant of all" (Mark 9:35)*. This paradox of leadership—that true greatness comes through service—challenges every worldly assumption about authority and power. The Messianic Man must embrace this paradox, understanding that his influence will be measured not by how many people serve him but by how faithfully he serves others.

The Kingdom of God awaits leaders who will reflect the character of the King. The Messianic Man must rise to this calling, leading with integrity, serving with love, and pointing others toward the ultimate Leader who gave His life for those He came to save. In doing so, he fulfills his highest purpose and contributes to the eternal work of God's kingdom on earth.

SYNOPSIS:

In this chapter, we have established the fundamental distinction between worldly leadership—characterized by superficial charisma, power-seeking, and self-promotion—and divine leadership—rooted in servanthood, humility, and sacrificial love. The Messianic Man is called to reject society's distorted view of authority and embrace God's blueprint for leadership, which emphasizes character over charisma and service over self-interest.

We have also explored how the Messianic Man must be integral in his leadership, demonstrating consistency between his private character and public actions. His responsibility extends to mentoring other men in righteousness, honor, and integrity, while leading women with wisdom, protection, and servant-hearted guidance. The educational component of his leadership involves developing both young men and women in spiritual maturity, practical skills, and cultural discernment.

Three dimensions of leadership are examined: spiritual leadership provides the foundation through relationship with God and teaching others; emotional leadership creates stability and wisdom during challenging circumstances; and physical leadership ensures provision, protection, and practical stewardship of resources. These dimensions must work in harmony to produce effective, godly leadership.

The contrasting examples of King David and King Saul illustrate the difference between leaders who seek God's heart despite personal failures and those who prioritize self-interest over divine will. David's authentic repentance and commitment to God's purposes made him effective despite his flaws, while Saul's pride and disobedience led to his downfall and the division of the kingdom.

Contemporary applications demonstrate how Messianic leadership principles apply across various roles—from judicial and executive positions to corporate leadership, legal advocacy, fatherhood, and marriage. In each context, the Messianic Man must integrate spiritual, emotional, and physical dimensions of leadership into his everyday life whenever the opportunity presents itself regardless of his position. He must be consistently searching for opportunities to lead and lead well—and almost all times, that may mean putting yourself last.

Will you lead like Saul—driven by pride, jealousy, and self-interest—or like David, a flawed yet repentant man after God's heart? The Messianic Leader chooses the latter, embracing accountability, courage, and grace. The world cries out for leaders who reflect Messiah—men of integrity, humility, and bold love. Will you answer the call? *"Whoever wants to be first must be last of all and servant of all" (Mark 9:35)*. Step into your God-given role, not for glory, but for the sake of those entrusted to you. The Kingdom needs you. Lead well.

CHAPTER FIVE: THE MESSIANIC HUSBAND

The World's Shallow Definition

In our contemporary landscape, society's blueprint for the "good husband" has become increasingly superficial and misguided. The modern cultural narrative paints an idealized picture of masculinity that revolves around financial prowess, domestic participation, and romantic gestures designed more for social media validation than genuine intimacy. This husband archetype is expected to surprise his wife with lavish gifts, participate in trending family activities, and maintain a carefully curated image of partnership that prioritizes appearances over substance.

This societal framework reduces the profound calling of husbandhood to a transactional relationship—a partnership based on material provision and emotional accommodation rather than spiritual leadership and sacrificial love. Popular culture celebrates the husband who defers to his wife's every whim, who leads through consensus rather than conviction, and who measures his success by his ability to maintain domestic harmony at any cost. While kindness and provision are not inherently wrong, this perspective fundamentally misunderstands the sacred nature of marriage and the husband's divine calling within it.

Such a worldview creates marriages built on shifting cultural trends rather than the unchanging foundation of God's Word. It produces relationships that may appear successful on the surface but lack the deep spiritual dimension that transforms two individuals into "one flesh" under God's design.

God's Design: The Husband as Covenant Leader

From God's eternal perspective, the role of a husband transcends societal expectations and enters the realm of sacred responsibility. Scripture presents the husband not as a mere partner in a contractual arrangement, but as the divinely appointed head of the household, called to lead with the same sacrificial love that Yeshua demonstrates toward His Bride, the Church.

The biblical husband is tasked with a threefold calling: to love unconditionally *(Ephesians 5:25-28)*, to lead sacrificially *(1 Peter 3:7)*, and to protect completely. This leadership is not characterized by domination or control, but by servant-hearted guidance that prioritizes his wife's spiritual, emotional, and physical flourishing above his own desires and comfort.

In *Ephesians 5:25*, Paul commands husbands to "love your wives, just as Messiah loved the church and gave himself up for her." This is not merely romantic affection or emotional attachment—it is agape love that seeks the highest good of another regardless of personal cost. Just as Yeshua sacrificed everything for His Bride's sanctification, the godly husband must be willing to lay down his life daily for his wife's growth in holiness and happiness.

The Hebrew and Greek languages provide profound insight into the biblical understanding of husbandhood. The Hebrew word "ba'al" (master, lord) reflects the husband's position of authority and responsibility within the household. This authority, however, is never meant to be tyrannical or oppressive. Rather, it carries the weight of accountability before God for the spiritual welfare of his family. The husband who truly understands his role as "ba'al" leads with the recognition that he will answer to the Almighty for how he has stewarded the precious souls entrusted to his care.

The Hebrew term "ish" (man) emphasizes the relational aspect of marriage—the beautiful complement between man (ish) and woman (ishah). This reveals that while the husband holds positional authority, marriage is fundamentally about partnership, mutual respect, and the unique ways that masculine and feminine natures reflect God's image together.

In the Greek New Testament, "aner" (husband/man) is used to describe the husband's specific role within the covenant relationship. When Paul uses this term in Ephesians 5, he is emphasizing that the husband's love should mirror Yeshua's love—sacrificial, sanctifying, and steadfast. The Greek word "kurios" (lord, master) further reinforces the husband's role as one who leads through service rather than domination, reflecting Yeshua's model of servant leadership.

The Husband's Sacred Service

Spiritual Leadership: The Priestly Calling

The Messianic husband serves as the spiritual priest of his household, bearing the responsibility to guide his wife and family toward deeper intimacy with the Almighty. This role encompasses several critical dimensions:

Prayer and Intercession: A godly husband regularly intercedes for his wife, praying not only for her immediate needs but for her spiritual growth, protection from temptation, and increasing intimacy with God. *1 Peter 3:7* warns that husbands who fail to honor their wives will find their prayers hindered, emphasizing the direct connection between marital harmony and spiritual effectiveness.

Teaching and Discipleship: As Adam was given God's commandments before Eve's creation, the husband bears the responsibility to teach and guide his wife in biblical truth. This involves regular study of Scripture together, discussing its application to daily life, and creating an environment where spiritual growth is prioritized and celebrated.

Sanctifying Love: Ephesians 5:26-27 reveals that husbands are called to love their wives "that he might sanctify her, having cleansed her by the washing of water with the word, that he might present the church to himself in splendor, without spot or wrinkle or any such thing, that she might be holy and without blemish." This means actively nurturing his wife's holiness, addressing sin with gentleness and wisdom, and creating an atmosphere where she feels safe to pursue righteousness without fear of condemnation.

Emotional Safeguarding: Building Unshakeable Security

The emotional dimension of a husband's service reflects the relational nature of God Himself. The husband is called to create emotional security through consistency, trustworthiness, and unwavering commitment.

Honoring Her as an Equal Image-Bearer: While roles within marriage may differ according to Scripture, both husband and wife are equally created in God's image *(Genesis 1:27)*. The godly husband honors his wife by valuing her insights, listening attentively to her concerns, and treating her with the dignity befitting a co-heir of God's grace.

Providing Emotional Security: *Proverbs 31:11* describes the virtuous woman whose "heart safely trusts in her husband." This trust is built through consistent actions, kept promises, and reliable character. The husband who demonstrates emotional security enables his wife to rest confidently in his leadership, knowing that his decisions are made with her best interests at heart.

Exercising Patience and Gentleness: *James 1:19* instructs believers to be "swift to hear, slow to speak, slow to wrath." The Messianic husband exemplifies this principle by responding to disagreements with patience rather than anger, seeking to understand before being understood, and maintaining gentleness even in moments of conflict.

Creating Space for Her Growth

A crucial aspect of godly husbandhood involves creating an environment where his wife can flourish in her God-given gifts and calling. This requires the husband to move beyond insecurity or competitiveness to genuine celebration of his wife's strengths and abilities.

The wise husband recognizes that his wife's growth and success does not diminish his own authority or significance. Instead, he understands that by encouraging her development, he is fulfilling his calling to present her as a mature, fully-realized woman of God. This involves identifying her spiritual gifts, encouraging her to use them for God's kingdom, and providing practical support for her growth.

He creates opportunities for her to exercise her gifts within appropriate biblical boundaries, celebrates her achievements, and provides the emotional safety necessary for her to take risks in faith. When she faces challenges or setbacks, he offers encouragement and wisdom rather than criticism or impatience.

Physical Provision and Intimacy

Material Provision: The husband's responsibility to provide for his family's material needs is clearly established in Scripture *(1 Timothy 5:8)*. However, this provision goes beyond mere financial support to encompass creating a home environment that promotes peace, security, and spiritual growth.

Physical Protection: The husband is called to be his wife's shield against physical danger and harm. This includes both obvious threats and subtle dangers, requiring vigilance and wisdom to anticipate and prevent potential harm. Adam clearly didn't do a great job with this seeing that He stood adjacent to his wife while the serpent tempted her and didn't intervene.

Sexual Intimacy: Scripture presents sexual intimacy within marriage as both a privilege and a responsibility. *1 Corinthians 7:3-5* makes clear that spouses have a duty to satisfy each other's sexual needs: *"Let the husband render to his wife the affection due her, and likewise also the wife to her husband. The wife does not have authority over her own body, but the husband does. And likewise the husband does not have authority over his own body, but the wife. Do not deprive one another except with consent for a time, that you may give yourselves to fasting and prayer; and come together again so that Satan does not tempt you because of your lack of self-control."*

The godly husband approaches sexual intimacy as an opportunity to express his deep love and commitment to his wife. He prioritizes her pleasure and satisfaction, viewing their physical union as a sacred communication of their covenant bond. This requires attentiveness to her needs, patience in learning what brings her joy, and consistency in expressing physical affection both within and outside the bedroom.

The Temptation of Child-Centered Marriage

One of the most subtle yet destructive threats to modern marriage is the tendency to prioritize children above the marital relationship. While this may seem noble or natural, it violates God's design for family structure and ultimately harms both the marriage and the children.

Scripture establishes marriage as the foundational relationship within the family unit. *Genesis 2:24* declares that a man shall *"leave his father and mother and be joined to his wife, and they shall become one flesh."* This divine order places the husband-wife relationship at the center of family life, with all other relationships flowing from this primary bond.

When children are elevated above the marriage, several destructive patterns emerge: the marital relationship becomes neglected and withered; children develop an unhealthy sense of entitlement and control; parents lose their unified authority and become divided in their parenting; and the children are robbed of the security that comes from witnessing a strong, loving marriage.

The godly husband maintains proper priorities by ensuring that his relationship with his wife remains the primary human relationship in his life. He demonstrates to his children what godly love looks like by treating their mother with honor, affection, and respect. He creates boundaries that protect marriage time and intimacy, understanding that the best gift he can give his children is parents who are deeply in love with each other.

Additionally, it is essential to intentionally set aside dedicated time for one's wife. This means that each day, the husband and wife should come together, fully immersing themselves in each other's presence. During this time, they ought to share the details of their day and engage in meaningful conversation. It is also an opportunity to nurture deeper emotional and physical intimacy, reaffirming their commitment to prioritizing one another.

While daily connection is vital, this practice should extend beyond routine moments. Husbands should also carve out special occasions for recreation and renewal with their wives—just the two of them. Whether through vacations, date nights, relaxation getaways, or even vow renewals, these intentional experiences strengthen the marital bond. Family outings are valuable, but the unique connection between husband and wife thrives when given undivided attention.

By making these moments a priority, a husband not only enriches his marriage but also reaffirms a powerful truth: out of all the people in the world, he chose her—and continues to choose her every day.

Protection: The Husband's Sacred Duty

The story of the Fall is not merely about disobedience—it is about failed leadership. When the serpent approached Eve, Adam's inaction set in motion humanity's ruin. Scripture reveals a sobering truth: Adam was not absent; he was passive. He stood beside Eve as she was deceived (Genesis 3:6), fully aware of God's command yet unwilling to intervene. His failure was not ignorance but abdication—a refusal to fulfill his role as protector and guide.

The Original Charge
Before Eve's creation, God entrusted Adam with two sacred responsibilities:
1. To cultivate and guard the Garden *(Genesis 2:15)*.
2. To obey a single prohibition— *"Of every tree you may freely eat, but of the Tree of the Knowledge of Good and Evil, you shall not eat, for in the day that you eat of it, you shall surely die" (Genesis 2:16-17).*

This command was given to Adam alone. Eve, formed later from his side, learned of it through him. Yet when tested, Adam did not reinforce God's word—he yielded to deception.

The Cost of Relinquished Duty
Adam's sin was not merely eating the fruit; it was his failure to lead. Consider the details:
- He was present during the temptation (Genesis 3:6).
- He heard Eve's misquoted version of God's command (Genesis 3:2-3) yet did not correct her.
- He chose compliance over courage, allowing his wife to assume the role of decision-maker—with catastrophic results.

The consequences were immediate and far-reaching: broken fellowship with God, a curse upon creation, and the introduction of suffering and death. But beneath the surface, a deeper lesson emerges: A man's neglect of his spiritual duty does not just affect him—it devastates those under his care.

The Husband's Sacred Role

Marriage, as God designed it, is not a democracy—it is a stewardship. A husband is called to:

1. **Protect**—not just physically, but spiritually, guarding his home against deception.

2. **Provide**—not merely materially, but with wisdom and clarity.

3. **Lead**—not as a tyrant, but as a servant accountable to God.

Adam's mistake was not that he listened to his wife—it was that he followed her into sin rather than leading her toward truth.

The Lesson for Modern Men

The Fall was not Eve's failure alone; it was Adam's dereliction of duty. Today, men face the same test: Will they remain passive, allowing culture, emotion, or convenience to dictate their choices? Or will they stand firm, upholding truth even when it is unpopular?

Leadership is not control—it is responsibility. And the man who embraces it does not merely save himself; he shields those he loves from the serpent's bite.

Spiritual Protection: The husband must guard his wife against spiritual deception by being grounded in Scripture himself and able to discern truth from error. He creates an environment where God's Word is central and false teachings are recognized and rejected.

Emotional Protection: The husband protects his wife emotionally by being her advocate, encouraging her during times of doubt, and shielding her from unnecessary criticism or harm. He builds her confidence through consistent affirmation and refuses to allow others to demean or disrespect her.

Physical Protection: The husband takes seriously his responsibility to safeguard his wife's physical well-being. This includes practical measures like home security, accompanying her when necessary, and being alert to potential dangers in their environment.

The Ministry of Reassurance

One of the most overlooked aspects of godly husbandhood is the continuous ministry of reassurance. Regardless of how often his wife needs affirmation, the wise husband provides it generously and consistently. This reflects Yeshua's constant reassurance of His love for His Bride.

Scripture provides numerous examples of this principle:

- *Ephesians 5:25-28* calls husbands to love their wives as their own bodies
- *Colossians 3:19* commands husbands to love their wives and not be harsh with them
- *Song of Solomon 4:7* demonstrates the husband's role in affirming his wife's beauty and worth

The husband's words have tremendous power to build up or tear down his wife's spirit. The godly husband uses this power to consistently communicate his love, appreciation, and commitment to his wife.

Biblical Example: Boaz as the Model Husband

Boaz provides an excellent example of biblical manhood and husbandhood in his relationship with Ruth. His character demonstrates several key qualities:

Protective Leadership: Boaz immediately took steps to protect Ruth when she came to glean in his fields, instructing his workers to ensure her safety and provision.

Generous Provision: He went beyond mere legal obligation to provide abundantly for Ruth's needs, demonstrating the heart of a provider.

Decisive Action: When the opportunity arose to redeem Ruth, Boaz acted quickly and decisively, handling the legal and social requirements with wisdom and integrity.

Honorable Treatment: Throughout their interactions, Boaz treated Ruth with dignity and respect, recognizing her character and worth.

Sacrificial Love: Boaz was willing to take on the responsibilities and potential complications of being Ruth's kinsman-redeemer, demonstrating selfless love.

The Failure of Passive Husbands

In contrast to Boaz's exemplary leadership, many modern husbands fall into the trap of passivity—much like Adam in the Garden. The passive husband fails to lead spiritually, makes decisions based on convenience rather than conviction, and avoids the difficult conversations and choices that true leadership requires.

This husband might appear peaceful and agreeable on the surface, but his failure to lead creates insecurity and confusion in his wife and children. His wife is forced to fill the leadership vacuum, often creating resentment and frustration as she is pushed into a role that doesn't align with her God-given design.

The passive husband's children grow up without a clear example of godly masculinity, leaving them unprepared for their own future roles as husbands and fathers. The family lacks the spiritual direction and protection that comes from strong, godly leadership.

Choosing a Godly Wife: The Foundation of Success

The wise man understands that choosing a godly wife is one of the most important decisions of his life. Proverbs 31:30 declares that "charm is deceptive, and beauty is fleeting; but a woman who fears the Lord is to be praised."

When seeking a wife, the godly man prioritizes:

Spiritual Maturity: She demonstrates a genuine relationship with God through prayer, Scripture study, and obedience to biblical principles.

Godly Character: She exhibits wisdom, diligence, kindness, and strength of character that will benefit the family and honor God.

Commitment to Biblical Roles: She embraces her calling as a wife and potential mother, understanding and accepting God's design for marriage and family.

Shared Vision: She shares his commitment to raising children according to biblical principles and building a home that honors God.

Emotional Maturity: She demonstrates the ability to handle conflict, stress, and the challenges of married life with grace and wisdom.

The process of choosing a wife requires prayer, wisdom, and patience. The man who rushes into marriage based on emotional attraction or social pressure often finds himself unequally yoked with someone who cannot fulfill the calling of biblical womanhood.

Capitalizing on Weaknesses and Strengths

A thriving marriage requires unity—both partners must align under biblical principles and trust in God's design for their union. As a

Messianic man, part of your role as leader is to recognize not only your own strengths and weaknesses but also those of your family. Once identified, you should leverage these qualities wisely for the household's benefit.

Practical Application:

Financial Stewardship: If you have a natural aptitude for managing money, take the lead in budgeting, investing, and planning for the family's future—not as a controlling figure, but as a faithful steward ensuring stability and growth. At the same time, if your wife has a sharp eye for spotting unnecessary expenses or finding better deals, defer to her judgment in those areas.

Household Responsibilities: If you are more skilled (or simply more available) to prepare meals, take initiative in the kitchen without waiting to be asked. If your wife has a gift for organization and keeping the home tidy, support her efforts rather than assuming she "should" handle all cleaning alone.

Parenting & Child Development: If your wife has a keen intuition about your children's emotional needs, trust her insights. If you excel in teaching discipline or practical skills, take ownership in those areas.

This approach fosters teamwork, ensuring that both partners contribute where they are most effective.

Listen to Your Wife

God often speaks through your wife in ways you may not immediately perceive. Marriage is designed so that neither spouse has all the answers—both must rely on each other's discernment. While the husband holds final authority, that authority is not a license to disregard his wife's wisdom. Instead, it should be exercised with humility, recognizing that her perspective may be the very guidance God is providing.

How to Apply This:

1. **Give Her Space to Speak:** When she shares concerns, ideas, or convictions, pause and truly listen—not just to respond, but to understand.
2. **Consider Her Input:** Even if your initial reaction is disagreement, weigh her words carefully. Ask yourself: Is there truth in what she's saying? Could God be using her to correct or refine my perspective?
3. **Make Decisions Together When Possible:** While some choices ultimately fall to you as the leader, seek unity whenever you can. A decision made in agreement is stronger than one imposed by authority alone.

Bad Example:

The Johnson family sat at the dinner table, the aroma of roasted chicken filling the air. Warren, their 12-year-old son, excitedly described a new recipe he had tried that afternoon. His mother smiled and turned to her husband.

"Honey, remember how you wanted to enroll Warren in karate next month? I've been thinking—he's always in the kitchen, experimenting with flavors. What if we signed him up for a kids' culinary program instead? He seems to really love it."

Mr. Johnson barely looked up from his plate. "No, karate will teach him discipline. Cooking is just a hobby."

"But he spends hours watching cooking shows," she pressed gently. "He even made dinner last week without being asked. Doesn't that show real passion?"

"I've already registered him," Mr. Johnson said firmly. "End of discussion."

The Problem:

- **Dismissiveness:** He didn't just disagree—he refused to engage with her reasoning at all.
- **Missed Opportunity:** Warren's culinary interest could have been a God-given gift, but his father's rigidity prevented exploration.
- **Marital Strain:** The wife felt silenced, as if her observations didn't matter. Over time, this breeds resentment.

Good Example:

The Carter family's dinner was lively, with 10-year-old Josephine describing her school project while James proudly passed around a plate of homemade cookies. Mrs. Carter glanced at her husband.

"Sweetheart, I know we talked about soccer for James, but have you noticed how much he enjoys cooking? He's been baking every weekend, and his teacher even mentioned his knack for flavors. Maybe we should consider a cooking class instead?"

Mr. Carter set down his fork, thoughtful. "You're right—he does seem passionate about it. I hadn't considered that." He turned to James. "Son, which would you rather do: karate or a cooking class?"

James's face lit up. "Cooking! I want to learn how to make desserts like Grandma's."

Mr. Carter nodded. "Then that's what we'll do. But let's also find a way to work on discipline, okay? Maybe we'll set up a little 'kitchen schedule' for you."

Mrs. Carter smiled. "I'd be happy to help with that."

Why This Works:

- **Active Listening:** The husband didn't just hear—he considered and validated his wife's observation.

- **Inclusive Decision-Making:** By involving Warren, they honored his God-given interests.
- **Balanced Leadership:** The father still guided the process (mentioning discipline) but with flexibility.

Conclusion

A godly marriage thrives when both spouses embrace their roles with humility and mutual respect. The husband leads not by domination, but by discernment—leveraging strengths, addressing weaknesses, and always listening for God's voice, even when it comes through his wife. When this balance is struck, the family flourishes, and God's design for marriage shines brightly.

Gifts

Mastering the Art of Biblical Gift-Giving as a Husband

Gift-giving is not merely an act of obligation—it is a sacred expression of love, attentiveness, and leadership. Many men, especially younger husbands, mistakenly believe that simply buying a gift (often at the last minute) fulfills their duty. But true, meaningful gift-giving runs much deeper. It requires wisdom, intentionality, and a heart attuned to your wife's needs—both spoken and unspoken.

The Difference Between Bad and Good Gift-Giving

A poor gift-giver operates out of duty rather than devotion. He buys his wife perfume she never wears because he didn't take time to learn her preferences. He gives her a generic card with no heartfelt words because he assumes the gift alone is enough. He waits until the last minute, scrambling to find something—anything—to check the box of "I got you something." His gifts are transactional, not transformational.

A masterful gift-giver, however, understands that the greatest gifts are not just material but spiritual and emotional. He pays attention to his wife's desires, struggles, and joys. He knows that true giving is not about the price tag but about the heart behind it. His gifts reflect *1 Peter 3:7,* which commands husbands to live with their wives *"in an understanding way,"* honoring them as co-heirs of God's grace.

Biblical Principles for Gift-giving

1. **Gifts Should Reflect Knowledge of Your Wife (Proverbs 31:10-11)**

- A wise husband studies his wife like a rare treasure. He knows her favorite scents, the books she loves, the small comforts that bring her peace.

- **Example:** If she loves gardening, a thoughtful gift isn't just flowers—it's a beautifully crafted journal for her to sketch plants, or a surprise day where you handle all chores so she can relax in her garden.

2. **Gifts Should Serve, Not Just Satisfy (Ephesians 5:25-28)**

- The Messiah gave Himself for the Church; husbands are called to sacrificial love. Sometimes the best "gift" is taking burdens off her shoulders.

- **Example:** If she's exhausted, the gift could be a clean home, a prepared meal, and putting the kids to bed so she can rest.

3. **Gifts Should Speak Her Love Language (Song of Solomon 2:4-5)**

- Does she value words of affirmation? A handwritten letter detailing why you cherish her. Quality time? A planned date without distractions. Acts of service? Handling a task she dreads.

- **Example:** If her love language is words, a simple necklace is nice—but pairing it with a love note she can read whenever she wears it makes it priceless.

4. **Gifts Should Be Given Cheerfully (2 Corinthians 9:7)**

- God loves a cheerful giver. Don't give resentfully or out of guilt. Let your gifts flow from a heart that delights in her joy.

Example of a Man Who Masters Gift-giving

The Thoughtful Husband:
Instead of buying his wife expensive jewelry she rarely wears, he notices how she lights up when talking about her childhood love of painting. For her birthday, he converts a spare room into a small art studio—complete with an easel, high-quality brushes, and a note: "Your creativity inspires me. This is your sacred space to dream again."

This gift shows:
- Observation (he knew her unspoken passion)
- Sacrifice (he invested time and effort, not just money)
- Encouragement (he nurtured her God-given gifts)

Final Challenge for Husbands
Gift-giving is not about perfection—it's about pursuit. Pursue knowing her. Pursue serving her. Pursue loving her as Messiah loves the Church. When you do, even the simplest gifts carry eternal weight. Your wife should feel God's provision over her through you, and feel safe in it.

"Every good gift and every perfect gift is from above..." (*James 1:17*)—may your gifts to your wife reflect the heart of the Ultimate Giver, since it reflects all of the blessings which Yeshua pours out to His bride a.k.a. the Church.

SYNOPSIS:

This chapter explored the sacred, often misunderstood role of a husband—contrasting society's shallow expectations (financial provision, emotional accommodation) with God's design (covenant leadership, sacrificial love). A husband's duty is threefold: to love like Messiah, lead like a servant, and protect like a guardian. His failure to embrace this role—whether through passivity (Adam), emotional neglect, or misplaced priorities—unleashes chaos in his home. True leadership isn't domination but stewardship: spiritual intercession, emotional security, and intentional intimacy. The enemy's goal? To distort marriage into a power struggle, obscuring the gospel it's meant to mirror.

"A man who fears the Lord does not seek a crown—he carries a cross. His strength is not in ruling, but in relinquishing; not in being served, but in serving unto death. For love is a blade that cuts the hand of the one who holds it, yet he grasps it tighter still."

Satan's Whisper: The Enemy's Strategy

"If I can convince the husband that his role is outdated, that submission is oppression, that leadership is toxic—then I can destroy the very foundation of God's design. When the husband becomes passive, the wife becomes frustrated; when the wife leads, the husband becomes emasculated. I will make them compete rather than complement, I will make them doubt rather than trust, I will make them focus on their rights rather than their responsibilities. For when marriage fails to reflect the relationship between the Messiah and His Church, I have succeeded in obscuring the very gospel itself. The husband who fails to lead sacrificially robs the world of seeing Yeshua. The husband who fails to love unconditionally prevents his wife from experiencing the depth of divine love. Let them settle for partnership without headship, affection without authority, coexistence without covenant—and I will have neutered the most powerful earthly testimony of eternal love." —The Adversary

This demonic strategy reveals the cosmic significance of the husband's role. The enemy understands that godly marriages are not merely human relationships but divine displays of the gospel message. When husbands fail to love sacrificially and lead courageously, they deprive the world of witnessing the beauty of Yeshua's love for His Bride. The stakes could not be higher—the husband's faithfulness to his calling impacts not only his family but the very proclamation of the gospel to a watching world.

The Messianic husband who understands these stakes will fight for his marriage with the same intensity that Yeshua fought for His Bride—through sacrifice, service, and unwavering commitment to God's perfect design.

CHAPTER SIX: THE MESSIANIC FATHER

Foundations of Biblical Fatherhood and Financial Stewardship

The Cultural Deception of Modern Fatherhood

Contemporary society has crafted an elaborate facade regarding the essence of godly fatherhood, one that prioritizes external manifestations over internal transformation. This cultural deception presents fatherhood through the lens of material achievement, career advancement, and visible participation in recreational activities. The modern paradigm celebrates the father who can furnish his children with luxury items, maintain consistent attendance at sporting events, or demonstrate professional success as the epitome of paternal excellence. While such demonstrations may reflect genuine care and dedication, they fundamentally misrepresent the profound spiritual responsibilities that define authentic biblical fatherhood.

The Scriptures present a dramatically different framework—one anchored in spiritual leadership, covenant faithfulness, and the transmission of divine wisdom across generations. The Scriptures illuminates this truth: *"Listen, my son, to your father's discipline, and do not forsake your mother's teaching"* (*Proverbs 1:8 TLV*). This passage reveals that true parental influence emanates not from material provision alone, but from the consistent impartation of divine truth and moral instruction.

The biblical model of fatherhood calls men to function as covenant representatives of the Almighty within their households, embodying His character while shepherding their families toward spiritual maturity. This chapter will examine how society's superficial metrics fail to address the deeper dimensions of fatherhood, particularly in the realm of financial stewardship and economic education, while establishing the scriptural foundation for raising children who possess both spiritual wisdom and practical life skills.

The Superficial Paradigm: Cultural Misperceptions of Fatherhood

Women's Misguided Search Criteria

When examining the qualities that contemporary women often prioritize in selecting potential fathers for their children, several troubling patterns emerge. These preferences, shaped by cultural narratives and media influence, frequently emphasize attributes that bear little correlation to authentic spiritual leadership or effective child-rearing capabilities.

Financial Security as Primary Criterion: Many women place disproportionate emphasis on a man's earning potential or material wealth, believing that financial resources alone constitute adequate provision for children. While economic stability serves as a practical necessity, this perspective often overlooks the deeper spiritual and emotional needs that children require for proper development. As Yeshua taught, *Do not worry, saying, 'What shall we eat?' or 'What shall we drink?' or 'What shall we wear?' For all these things the Gentiles eagerly seek. But your heavenly Father knows that you need all these things. But seek first the kingdom and His righteousness, and all these things shall be added to you* **(Matthew 6:31-33 TLV)**.

Physical Dominance Over Spiritual Authority: Cultural narratives perpetuate the myth that physical strength or aggressive dominance equals effective leadership. This misconception leads women to seek men who project external power while potentially lacking the spiritual authority that comes from submission to the Almighty. True biblical authority flows from humble obedience to divine commandments, not from human intimidation tactics.

Charismatic Appeal Versus Character Depth: The attraction to socially charismatic men often overshadows the evaluation of deeper character qualities. Charm and confidence may create temporary appeal, but they provide no foundation for the consistent moral guidance that children require throughout their developmental years.

The Pendulum of Weakness: A particularly damaging trend involves women who, having encountered overly controlling men, swing to the opposite extreme by seeking emotionally passive or spiritually weak partners. This creates households where proper spiritual leadership is absent, ultimately affecting the children's understanding of divine order and family structure.

Physical Attraction Over Spiritual Compatibility: While physical attraction maintains its legitimate place in marital relationships, the rejection of spiritually qualified men based solely on physical appearance represents a profound misunderstanding of lasting marital success and effective parenting. Too many times we hear women claim, "he's not six feet tall, so I don't want him," or "he's not black, so I don't want him," or "he doesn't dress good, so I'll pass on him." These women aren't seeking the deeper things in a man such as character, principles, faith, and personality. Therefore, they miss out on the potential blessing which God has cultivated in him through the Messiah. As men, it is important to recognize women of such types and stay clear.

The Biblical Standard: God's Perspective on Fatherhood

Spiritual Leadership as Foundation

The Scriptures establish spiritual leadership as the cornerstone of effective fatherhood. *"And you shall love Adonai your God with all your heart and with all your soul and with all your strength. These words, which I am commanding you today, are to be on your heart. You are to teach them diligently to your children, and speak of them when you sit in your house, when you walk by the way, when you lie down and when you rise up" (Deuteronomy 6:5-7 TLV).*

This passage reveals that godly fathers must first establish their own intimate relationship with the Almighty before attempting to guide their children spiritually. The Hebrew concept of shamayim (heaven) begins in the home, where fathers serve as earthly representatives of divine authority and wisdom.

A Messianic father demonstrates spiritual leadership through:

Daily Spiritual Disciplines: Maintaining consistent prayer, Torah study, and worship practices that children can observe and emulate. *"But as for me and my house, we will serve Adonai" (Joshua 24:15 TLV).*

Teaching Divine Truth: Actively instructing children in biblical principles, not merely delegating this responsibility to religious institutions. The father serves as the primary spiritual educator within the household.

Modeling Covenant Faithfulness: Demonstrating unwavering commitment to biblical principles, even when such commitment requires personal sacrifice or cultural opposition.

Love Expressed Through Sacrifice

Biblical fatherhood manifests itself through self-sacrificial love that mirrors the Messiah's devotion to His people. *"Husbands, love your wives just as Messiah also loved His community and gave Himself up for her" (Ephesians 5:2).* It is a principle already spoken for the wife, but it also extends to fatherhood, where men must prioritize their children's welfare above personal comfort or convenience.

Such sacrificial love includes:

Time Investment: Dedicating significant portions of personal time to child development, education, and relationship building, even when career or recreational activities present competing demands.

Emotional Availability: Creating safe environments where children feel secure expressing their thoughts, fears, and aspirations without judgment or dismissal.

Patient Instruction: Providing consistent guidance through multiple explanations and demonstrations, recognizing that children require repetition and patience to internalize important concepts.

Character Development Over Achievement

The biblical model prioritizes character formation over external achievement. *"The path of the righteous is like the light of dawn, shining brighter and brighter until full day* **(Proverbs 4:18 TLV).** Godly fathers focus on developing their children's moral foundations rather than merely pursuing academic or athletic accomplishments.

This involves:

Integrity Training: Teaching children to speak truthfully, honor commitments, and maintain consistent behavior regardless of external pressures or temptations.

Humility Cultivation: Modeling and teaching proper submission to divine authority while demonstrating confidence in God-given abilities and responsibilities.

Compassion Development: Instructing children in mercy, kindness, and concern for others' welfare, particularly those in vulnerable circumstances.

Selecting a Godly Partner: The Foundation of Family Success

Biblical Criteria for Spouse Selection

The selection of a suitable wife represents one of the most crucial decisions affecting a man's ability to fulfill his role as a godly father. The Scriptures provide clear guidance regarding the qualities that characterize an excellent wife and mother: *"A woman of valor, who can find? Her value is far above rubies"* **(Proverbs 31:10 TLV).**

Spiritual Compatibility: The prospective wife must demonstrate genuine faith in Yeshua as Messiah and commitment to biblical principles. *"Do not be unequally yoked with unbelievers. For what partnership does righteousness have with lawlessness? Or what fellowship does light have with darkness?"* **(2 Corinthians 6:14 TLV).**

Submission to Divine Order: She must understand and embrace the biblical structure of family hierarchy, recognizing the husband's role as spiritual leader while fulfilling her own calling as helper and encourager. *"However, let each one of you love his own wife as himself, and let the wife respect her husband"* **(Ephesians 5:33 TLV).**

Character Qualities: Seeking a woman who demonstrates kindness, wisdom, self-control, and devotion to serving others rather than pursuing selfish ambitions.

Shared Vision: Ensuring alignment regarding family goals, child-rearing philosophies, and long-term spiritual objectives.

Warning Against Problematic Partnerships

The wisdom literature provides explicit warnings regarding women who would undermine family stability and spiritual growth. *"It is better to live in a corner of a roof than in a house shared with a contentious woman"* **(Proverbs 21:9 TLV).** *"It is better to live in a* *desert land than with a quarrelsome and irritable woman"* **(Proverbs 21:19 TLV)**.

These passages emphasize that marital harmony directly affects children's emotional and spiritual development. A contentious or rebellious wife creates household tension that inevitably influences children's understanding of divine order and family relationships.

Financial Stewardship: Developing Children's Economic Wisdom

The Biblical Foundation of Financial Education

One of the most neglected aspects of modern faith-driven parenting involves the comprehensive training of children in biblical financial principles. The Scriptures contain extensive guidance regarding money management, economic stewardship, and the proper relationship between material resources and spiritual priorities.

"For the love of money is a root of all kinds of evil—some, longing for it, have gone astray from the faith and pierced themselves through with many sorrows" (1 Timothy 6:10 TLV). This passage reveals that children must learn to view money as a tool for serving divine purposes rather than as an end in itself.

Establishing Financial Intelligence in Children

Early Introduction to Economic Concepts: Beginning around age five or six, children should receive age-appropriate instruction regarding money's function, value, and proper use. This includes understanding the relationship between work and compensation, the importance of proper saving, and the biblical mandate for generous giving.

Practical Application Through Household Responsibilities: Assigning children specific chores or responsibilities that result in monetary compensation teaches the fundamental principle that resources are earned through diligent effort. *"In all toil there is profit, but mere talk tends only to poverty* **(Proverbs 14:23 TLV)**.

Budgeting and Planning Skills: Teaching children to allocate their resources across multiple categories—giving, saving, investing, and spending—develops crucial decision-making abilities that will serve them throughout their adult lives.

Investment Principles: As children mature, introducing concepts of compound interest, long-term planning, and wise investment strategies prepares them for financial independence and effective stewardship of family resources. This includes educating them on business accounts, taxes, IRA's, High-Yield Savings Accounts, Brokerage Accounts, HSA's, etc. This also includes the stock market.

The Tithe as Financial Foundation

Perhaps the most fundamental financial principle that children must learn involves the priority of giving to the Almighty. *"Bring the whole tithe into the storehouse, so that there may be food in My house. Test Me now in this, says Adonai-Tzva'ot, if I will not open for you the windows of heaven and pour out for you a blessing until there is not enough room"* **(Malachi 3:10 TLV)**.

Children should understand that a portion of all income belongs to God, not as a burdensome obligation, but as recognition of His ownership over all resources. This principle establishes the proper relationship between material wealth and spiritual priorities while demonstrating trust in divine provision. Whether through homeless giving, or simple acts of random kindness, God must be instilled in the child's mind so as he grows he gives.

Practical Implementation:
- Teaching children to set aside ten percent of any money they receive before considering other uses

- Explaining how tithing demonstrates obedience to divine commandments
- Showing how generous giving results in divine blessing and provision
- Modeling consistent tithing behavior for children to observe

Developing Entrepreneurial Skills

The biblical narrative celebrates industrious individuals who create value through their talents and efforts. *"She considers a field and buys it. From her earnings she plants a vineyard"* **(Proverbs 31:16 TLV).** Children should be encouraged to develop entrepreneurial thinking and creative problem-solving abilities. This starts with observation from the father. As a Messianic Man, your job is to be aware of your child's gifts and capabilities while they are young, and help them build that skill all the way up into their adulthood. If your five year old can play the piano well, consider finding them a skilled teacher. If they are intrigued at the idea of cooking, cultivate that skill in them. As they grow, the skill won't depart from them. Who knows, that skill may just be what generates their wealth in the long run.

Age-Appropriate Business Ventures:

- Elementary age: Simple ventures like lemonade stands, pet-sitting, or helping neighbors with basic tasks
- Middle school: More complex projects involving product creation, service provision, or small-scale retail operations
- High school: Formal business planning, marketing strategies, and financial record-keeping

Key Principles to Teach:
- Identifying market needs and developing solutions
- Understanding profit margins and expense management

- Building reputation through excellent service and integrity
- Reinvesting profits for business growth and expansion
- Learning how to be completely aware of what's going on in the world

Teaching Financial Discipline and Delayed Gratification

Modern consumer culture promotes immediate satisfaction and impulse purchasing, directly contradicting biblical principles of patience and careful planning. *"The plans of the diligent lead surely to abundance, but everyone who is hasty comes surely to poverty" (Proverbs 21:5 TLV).*

Strategies for Developing Financial Discipline:

Goal-Setting Exercises: Helping children identify specific items they want to purchase and calculating how long they must save to afford them. This process teaches patience while demonstrating the relationship between effort and reward.

Comparison Shopping: Teaching children to research prices across multiple vendors before making purchases, developing critical thinking skills while maximizing resource efficiency.

Quality Over Quantity: Emphasizing the value of purchasing well-made items that will last longer rather than cheaper alternatives that require frequent replacement. They must develop a habit of asking themselves "what is the value of this?" or "how will this help me make more money?" when comforted with an opportunity to spend.

Emergency Fund Concepts: Even young children can understand the importance of setting aside money for unexpected needs, developing security and wise planning habits.

Understanding Debt and Credit

As children approach adolescence, they must receive thorough education regarding debt, credit, and financial obligations. The Scriptures provide clear warnings about the dangers of indebtedness: *"The rich rule over the poor, and the borrower is slave to the lender" (Proverbs 22:7 TLV).*

Essential Concepts to Address:

Interest Calculations: Teaching children how compound interest works in both positive (savings/investments) and negative (debt) contexts.

Credit Score Implications: Explaining how financial decisions affect long-term borrowing ability and overall economic opportunities.

Avoiding Consumer Debt: Emphasizing the importance of living within one's means and avoiding purchases that cannot be afforded with current resources.

Strategic Debt Usage: When appropriate, discussing how certain types of debt (such as real estate or education) can serve as investments in future earning capacity. Not all debt is bad debt.

Comprehensive Child Development: Beyond Financial Education

Academic Excellence as Stewardship

While financial education forms a crucial component of child development, godly fathers must maintain comprehensive oversight of their children's academic progress. Educational achievement represents stewardship of the intellectual gifts that the Almighty has provided. *"Whatever you do, work heartily, as for the Lord and not for men" (Colossians 3:23 TLV).*

Daily Academic Engagement:
- Reviewing homework assignments and providing assistance when needed
- Communicating regularly with teachers regarding academic progress and behavioral issues
- Encouraging excellence while maintaining realistic expectations based on individual abilities
- Celebrating achievements while emphasizing the importance of consistent effort over natural talent

Critical Thinking Development:
- Teaching children to evaluate information sources and identify bias or misinformation
- Encouraging questions and independent research on topics of interest
- Developing logical reasoning skills through discussion and debate
- Emphasizing the compatibility between faith and intellectual pursuit

Spiritual Formation and Religious Education

The transmission of spiritual truth represents the father's primary responsibility and greatest privilege. *"Train up a child in the way he should go; even when he is old he will not depart from it* **(Proverbs 22:6 TLV)**.

Structured Religious Instruction:
Beginning around age five, children should receive formal instruction in biblical narratives, moral principles, and theological concepts which includes Torah (or the 613 laws within the first five books of the Bible). This education must be systematic and progressive,

building upon previously learned foundations while introducing more complex spiritual truths as children mature intellectually.

Personal Relationship Development:
Beyond intellectual knowledge, children must be encouraged to develop their own personal relationship with the Almighty through prayer, worship, and meditation on Scripture. Fathers should model this intimate connection while providing guidance for their children's spiritual development.

Community Involvement:
Regular participation in synagogue or congregational activities provides children with broader spiritual community while reinforcing household religious instruction.

Sexual Purity and Relationship Education

One of the most crucial yet commonly neglected aspects of child development involves comprehensive education regarding sexuality, purity, and proper relationships. The cultural taboo surrounding these topics has resulted in children receiving their primary education from unreliable sources, often resulting in distorted understanding and inappropriate behavior.

Age-Appropriate Sexual Education:
Early Childhood (Ages 5-8): Basic understanding of physical differences between males and females, proper names for body parts, and the concept of personal boundaries and appropriate touch. This even includes instilling the concept of God and how our bodies are temples of the Most High. Therefore, it must be treated with care according to scripture.

Pre-Adolescence (Ages 9-12): Detailed explanation of puberty, physical changes, and emotional development. Deeper emphasis of biblical principles regarding purity and the sacred nature of sexuality within marriage.

Adolescence (Ages 13-17): Comprehensive discussion of sexual temptation, dating relationships, courtship principles, and preparation for marriage. Emphasis on maintaining purity until marriage and selecting a godly spouse.

Biblical Foundation for Sexuality:

Children must understand that sexuality represents a divine gift designed for expression within the covenant of marriage. *"Marriage is to be honored by all, and the marriage bed is to be kept undefiled" (Hebrews 13:4 TLV).* It is a unity between two married individuals. When two come together, God said 'yes.'

Children must also be educated in the concept of heterosexuality. By no means should the sin of homosexuality creep into the household. This requires vigilance of who the child hangs around and intervening when friendships become suspicious. Suspicious friendships are friendships that start to show signs of disobedience to God, especially when they start to become more deliberate. When such things become evident, it is time to make the child aware of such friendships and attempt to edify their friend. If edification isn't possible, then its time to forbid interactions with the person.

Practical Boundaries:

- Guidelines for appropriate physical interaction in dating relationships
- Strategies for avoiding compromising situations

- Understanding the emotional and spiritual consequences of sexual impurity
- Developing accountability relationships with godly mentors

Discipline: The Art of Loving Correction

Biblical Principles of Child Discipline

The Scriptures provide extensive guidance regarding the proper discipline of children, emphasizing both the necessity of correction and the importance of maintaining appropriate methods and motivations. *Discipline your son while there is hope, but do not set your heart on his destruction* **(Proverbs 19:18 TLV)**.

Discipline Rooted in Divine Standards:
Effective discipline focuses on violations of divine commandments rather than arbitrary parental preferences. Children should understand that they are being corrected for transgressing God's moral standards, not merely for inconveniencing their parents.

Consistency and Fairness:
Disciplinary measures must be applied consistently across all children and circumstances. Favoritism or mood-dependent discipline creates confusion and resentment while undermining parental authority.

Restoration as Goal:
The ultimate objective of discipline involves restoration of fellowship and character development rather than punishment for its own sake. *"No discipline seems pleasant at the time, but painful. Later on, however, it produces a harvest of righteousness and peace for those who have been trained by it* **(Hebrews 12:11 TLV)**.

Balancing Firmness with Mercy

While maintaining standards remains crucial, godly fathers must also demonstrate mercy and understanding, recognizing their own past failures and the grace they have received from the Almighty. Adonai, do not rebuke me in Your anger, nor discipline me in Your wrath *(Psalm 6:1 TLV)*.

Measured Response:

The severity of disciplinary action should correspond appropriately to the offense committed while considering the child's age, maturity level, and previous behavior patterns.

Teaching Moments:

Every disciplinary situation provides an opportunity for instruction regarding biblical principles, character development, and the consequences of moral choices.

Forgiveness and Restoration:

Following appropriate discipline, fathers should clearly communicate forgiveness and restoration of relationship, modeling the divine pattern of judgment followed by mercy.

Identifying and Meeting Children's Needs

Comprehensive Needs Assessment

Effective fathers develop keen observation skills that enable them to identify their children's physical, emotional, and spiritual needs, even when children cannot articulate these needs themselves. This ability requires consistent attention and genuine concern for each child's welfare.

Physical Needs Recognition:
- Adequate nutrition, sleep, and exercise requirements
- Medical attention for illness or injury
- Appropriate clothing and shelter

- Safety and protection from harmful influences

Emotional Needs Assessment:
- Need for affection, encouragement, and validation
- Desire for individual attention and quality time
- Requirement for security and stability
- Processing of fears, anxieties, and developmental challenges

Spiritual Needs Identification:
- Hunger for meaning and purpose
- Questions regarding faith and divine truth
- Need for moral guidance and character development
- Desire to understand their identity in relation to the Almighty

Responsive Parenting Strategies

Once needs are identified, godly fathers must respond appropriately and promptly. Delayed or inadequate response to legitimate needs can result in behavioral problems, emotional difficulties, and spiritual confusion.

Proactive Communication:
Regular one-on-one conversations with each child provide opportunities for need identification while strengthening relationship bonds.

Environmental Assessment:
Creating home environments that support healthy development while removing obstacles to spiritual and emotional growth.

Individual Attention:
Recognizing that each child possesses unique needs, abilities, and developmental patterns that require individualized approaches. Focus on not dumping excessive attention on one child thereby blotting out attention from others. This will lead to insecurity

developments in the favored child's siblings. Then, you'll have a Joseph and his brothers situation all over again.

Practical Implementation: Daily Rhythms of Godly Fatherhood

Morning Spiritual Leadership

Beginning each day with spiritual focus sets the tone for family life and demonstrates paternal priorities. In the morning, Adonai, You hear my voice. In the morning I lay my requests before You and wait in expectation *(Psalm 5:3 TLV)*.

Family Devotional Time:
- Brief Scripture reading appropriate for children's ages
- Prayer for family needs and daily guidance
- Discussion of biblical principles and their practical application

Personal Modeling:
Children should observe their father's personal devotional practices, understanding that spiritual leadership begins with individual commitment to divine relationship.

Educational Oversight and Financial Training

Homework Review Sessions:
Regular assessment of academic progress while providing assistance and encouragement for challenging subjects. Simply saying "do your homework" isn't sufficient. Occasionally check-in with you child's academic progress and assist them wherever they need the help.

Financial Education Integration:

- Weekly discussions about budgeting, saving, and spending decisions
    - Practical exercises involving money management and planning
    - Regular review of children's financial goals and progress

Life Skills Development:

Teaching practical abilities such as cooking, cleaning, basic maintenance, and organization that will serve children throughout their adult lives.

Evening Reflection and Blessing

Daily Debriefing:

Conversations about daily experiences, challenges, and lessons learned provide opportunities for guidance and relationship building.

Bedtime Blessings:

Following the biblical pattern of patriarchal blessing, fathers should regularly speak words of affirmation and spiritual blessing over their children.

Gratitude Practices:

Teaching children to acknowledge divine blessings and express thanksgiving for daily provisions and protection.

Long-Term Vision: Raising World-Changers

Generational Impact

Effective fatherhood extends beyond immediate family to influence future generations and broader communities. One generation will commend Your works to another, and will declare Your mighty acts **(Psalm 145:4 TLV).**

Legacy Thinking:

Decisions regarding child-rearing should consider their impact on grandchildren and subsequent generations, not merely immediate convenience or results.

Community Influence:

Children raised according to biblical principles become positive influences within their communities, advancing divine kingdom purposes through their character and abilities.

Preparing Children for Leadership

Godly fathers must prepare their children to assume leadership roles within their own families and communities. This preparation involves developing both spiritual maturity and practical competence.

Leadership Skill Development:
- Decision-making abilities under pressure
- Communication skills for teaching and persuasion
- Problem-solving capabilities for complex challenges
- Servant leadership attitudes that prioritize others' welfare

Spiritual Authority Training:
- Deep knowledge of Scripture and theological principles
- Personal relationship with the Almighty through prayer and worship
- Character qualities that earn respect and trust
- Vision for advancing divine purposes in their generation

The Playful Patriarch: How a Father's Presence Shapes Souls

There is a silent crisis in modern fatherhood—one that goes unnoticed because its wounds are not always visible. It is the crisis of the absent father, not merely in body, but in spirit. He may be present in the home, yet emotionally distant, a specter of authority who rules with discipline but never delights, who corrects but never connects. His children grow like untended vines—twisted, searching for light in all the wrong places, their hearts starved for the warmth of a father's joy.

This is not the way of the Messianic father.

The Scriptures speak of a God who rejoices over His children with singing *(Zephaniah 3:17)*, who numbers the hairs on their heads *(Luke 12:7)*, who draws them near with open arms *(Luke 15:20)*. A father who reflects this divine love does not merely instruct—he engages. He does not merely command—he invites. And one of the most powerful, yet neglected, ways he does this is through play.

The Cost of a Father Who Never Plays

Consider two fathers—one a ghost, the other a guide.

The Ghost Father

He is a man of stern words and heavy hands. He believes affection makes children weak, that laughter undermines authority. His home is a place of rules without relationship, where children speak only when spoken to, where emotions are locked away like shameful secrets.

- His son grows into a man who cannot connect, who views tenderness as a flaw. He either dominates those beneath him or shrinks from all confrontation, never having learned the balance of strength and love.

- His daughter, aching for male affirmation, seeks it in the arms of boys who do not cherish her, mistaking attention for love.

Proverbs 17:22 (TLV) warns: *"A joyful heart is good medicine, but a broken spirit dries up the bones."*

The ghost father does not realize that in his refusal to play, to laugh, to be present in joy, he has broken his children's spirits long before the world ever could.

The Guiding Father

He is a man who understands that play is the language of childhood, and he is fluent in it. He wrestles with his sons, not just to teach them strength, but to show them that authority does not have to be cruel. He dances with his daughters, not out of obligation, but to imprint upon their souls that they are worthy of a father's delight.

- When he corrects, his children listen—because they trust him.
- When they fail, they run to him, not from him—because they know his love is not conditional on perfection.
- When the world tells them they are worthless, they do not believe it—because their father's laughter, his roughhousing, his silly songs, have already whispered a deeper truth: "You are mine, and I rejoice in you."

The Dark Truth of Play's Absence

A child who has never known his father's joy will:
- Shut down emotionally, believing vulnerability is dangerous.
- Struggle with authority, seeing it as something to resist or fear, never something to respect.
- Seek counterfeit affirmation—through reckless behavior, toxic relationships, or the hollow approval of strangers.

This is not mere sentimentality—it is spiritual warfare. The enemy thrives in silent homes where fathers mistake severity for righteousness, where children grow into adults who cannot fathom a Heavenly Father who delights in them.

The Way Forward: Becoming a Father Who Plays with Purpose

1. Initiate Play Without Agenda

- A father who shoots hoops with his son, not to critique his form, but simply to be with him, teaches more about God's unconditional love than any sermon.

2. Laugh Often

- A home without laughter is a home under siege. The father who can mock his own mistakes teaches his children that failure is not fatal.

3. Use Play to Teach

- A game of chess becomes a lesson in patience. A wrestling match becomes a lesson in controlled strength. A silly story at bedtime becomes a lesson in creativity.

4. Let Them See Your Joy in Them

- A child who hears his father's laughter at his jokes, who feels his father's arms around him in victory and defeat, will never question whether he is loved.

Conclusion: The Eternal Echo of a Father's Laughter

The world is full of men who were never fathered well—who now repeat the cycle of distance and discipline without delight. But the Messianic father breaks this curse. He understands that play is not frivolous—it is foundational. It is the bridge between authority and affection, between law and love.

When a father plays with his child, he does more than create a memory—he shapes a soul. He teaches his son how to lead with joy. He teaches his daughter what love looks like. And most importantly, he shows them, in flesh and blood, the heart of a Father in Heaven who does not merely tolerate them—but rejoices over them with singing.

Psalm 127:3, 5, TLV

"Behold, children are a heritage from the Lord... Blessed is the man whose quiver is full of them."

A man who masters this—who is both strong and joyful, firm and playful—does not just raise children. He raises heirs of the Kingdom.

SYNOPSIS: The Eternal Significance of Godly Fatherhood

The role of father represents one of the most significant responsibilities that a man can assume, carrying implications that extend far beyond temporal concerns into eternal consequences. The difference between superficial cultural fatherhood and biblical paternal leadership affects not only immediate family welfare but also the spiritual trajectory of future generations.

Contemporary society's emphasis on material provision and external achievement, while containing elements of legitimate concern, fundamentally misrepresents the deeper spiritual dimensions of effective fatherhood. True success in parenting cannot be measured merely by children's academic achievements, athletic accomplishments, or material prosperity, though these outcomes may accompany proper spiritual training.

The biblical model calls fathers to function as covenant representatives of the Almighty within their households, demonstrating His character while training children in divine truth and practical wisdom. This comprehensive approach encompasses spiritual instruction, financial education, character development, academic oversight, and relationship guidance, all grounded in the foundation of personal submission to divine authority.

The selection of a godly wife represents a crucial component of successful fatherhood, as her character and spiritual commitment directly influence children's development and the overall household atmosphere. The wisdom literature's warnings regarding contentious or rebellious women reflect the understanding that marital harmony provides the essential foundation for effective child-rearing.

Financial education, often neglected in contemporary faith-driven households, represents a vital component of comprehensive child development. Teaching children biblical principles of stewardship, generosity, and wise resource management prepares them for adult responsibilities while establishing proper relationships between material wealth and spiritual priorities.

The discipline of children, when conducted according to biblical principles, serves as an expression of love that guides moral development and character formation. Balanced approaches that combine appropriate firmness with mercy and restoration model divine justice while promoting healthy relationship patterns.

Perhaps most importantly, godly fathers must develop the ability to identify and respond to their children's comprehensive needs—physical, emotional, and spiritual. This requires consistent attention, genuine concern, and the wisdom to discern underlying issues that children may not be able to articulate independently.

The eternal significance of biblical fatherhood extends beyond individual families to influence entire communities and future generations. Children raised according to divine principles become agents of positive change within their spheres of influence, advancing the purposes of the Almighty's kingdom through their character, abilities, and spiritual commitment.

As Messianic men embrace the calling of fatherhood, they must reject cultural deceptions that minimize the spiritual dimensions of this sacred responsibility. Instead, they must pursue the biblical standard that calls them to represent divine character while shepherding their families toward spiritual maturity and practical competence.

The investment of time, energy, and resources required for godly fatherhood represents a costly commitment that often conflicts with personal preferences and cultural expectations. However, the eternal rewards of raising children who know and serve the Almighty far exceed any temporal sacrifices required to fulfill this divine calling.

Behold, children are a heritage from Adonai, the fruit of the womb a reward **(Psalm 127:3 TLV)**. This truth reminds fathers that their children represent gifts from the Almighty, entrusted to their care for training in righteousness and preparation for eternal purposes. The faithful execution of this responsibility constitutes one of the highest forms of worship and service that a man can offer to his Creator.

The path of biblical fatherhood demands supernatural wisdom, strength, and patience that can only be obtained through intimate relationship with the Almighty. As fathers commit themselves to this divine standard, they discover that the same God who calls them to this responsibility also provides the resources necessary for its successful fulfillment.

In a generation marked by confusion regarding family structure and parental responsibilities, godly fathers serve as beacons of divine truth, demonstrating through their lives and households the beauty and effectiveness of the Creator's design for family life. Their faithfulness in this calling contributes to the restoration of biblical values within their communities while preparing the next generation to continue advancing the purposes of the Almighty's kingdom.

As for me and my house, we will serve Adonai **(Joshua 24:15 TLV)**. This declaration must characterize every Messianic father's commitment, establishing the foundation upon which all other aspects of family life are built and from which all future generations will benefit.

CHAPTER SEVEN: THE MESSIANIC MAN AS A BUILDER

In today's world, society often defines a "builder" as someone who constructs physical structures, establishes businesses, or creates wealth and influence. These individuals are celebrated for their ability to shape the material world through innovation, entrepreneurship, and leadership. Society tends to equate building with tangible achievements—constructing skyscrapers, founding companies that generate wealth, or creating technological advancements that revolutionize industries. Builders in this sense are often admired for their ambition and ability to leave behind visible legacies that symbolize power and success.

However admirable these accomplishments may be in the eyes of society, they often focus solely on external results rather than internal transformation or moral responsibility. The societal concept of building frequently neglects the importance of character development or spiritual accountability in favor of measurable outcomes like profit margins or social status.

The Bible offers a profoundly different perspective on what it means to be a builder, particularly in the context of manhood and community. A biblical builder is not merely someone who constructs with bricks and mortar but someone who builds lives, relationships, faith, and communities according to God's principles. This distinction challenges men to reflect on whether they are building for worldly recognition or eternal significance.

To be a biblical builder is to align one's life with God's design and purpose and bring it into existence through creativity. It involves using words, actions, and resources to edify others while advancing God's kingdom on earth. A man can become a biblical builder by embodying Messiah-like qualities such as humility, service, integrity, and love. By prioritizing spiritual growth over material success and focusing on uplifting others rather than self-promotion, he can leave a lasting impact on his family, community, and beyond.

Exegetical Breakdown of a Biblical Builder

The concept of a "builder" in the Bible carries both literal and metaphorical meanings. In Hebrew, the word for builder is often derived from the root word "banah" which means "to build, construct, or establish." This term is used not only to describe physical construction but also metaphorically to signify establishing families, communities, or spiritual legacies. For example, in Genesis 2:22, God "built" (banah) Eve from Adam's rib, emphasizing the creative and foundational role of building.

In biblical theology, a builder is someone who participates in creating or establishing something that aligns with God's purposes. Builders are often seen as stewards of God's plans—whether constructing physical structures like the Temple or metaphorically building lives and communities rooted in faith and obedience to God.

The Hebrew term "banah" reflects more than just physical labor; it conveys intentionality and purpose. In ancient Israelite culture, building was deeply tied to covenantal relationships with God. Physical construction often symbolized obedience to God's commands, as seen in Noah building the ark *(Genesis 6:14-22)* and Solomon constructing the Temple *(1 Kings 6)*. Spiritual building involves establishing households or legacies aligned with God's will, as emphasized in **Psalm 127:1:** *"Unless Adonai builds the house, those who build it labor in vain."*

What the Bible Says About Being a Builder

In contrast to society's view of building as an external endeavor focused on material success, the Bible emphasizes internal transformation and spiritual construction as the foundation for true building. According to Scripture, being a builder involves creating something lasting in alignment with God's will—whether nurturing relationships within one's family (Ephesians 5:25-33), fostering unity within the church *(1 Corinthians 3:9-11)*, or serving others selflessly *(Matthew 20:26-28)*.

The Bible also highlights Yeshua Messiah as the ultimate model for builders. Referred to metaphorically as both a carpenter, particularly a stone mason *(Mark 6:3)* and the chief cornerstone *(Ephesians 2:20)*, Yeshua exemplified how men should build their lives upon solid foundations rooted in faith rather than fleeting worldly pursuits *(Matthew 7:24-27)*. His ministry was centered around building people up spiritually—healing brokenness, teaching truth with authority, and demonstrating sacrificial love.

The Divine Call to Prosperity Through Work

A foundational truth that permeates Scripture is that poverty is not God's will for those who believe in Him. As stated in *3 John 1:2 (TLV)*, "Beloved, I pray that in all respects you may prosper and be in good health, just as your soul prospers." This prosperity, however, is not pursued through greed or exploitation but through diligent work, wise stewardship, and faithful service to Adonai.

The Messianic man understands that wealth is not inherently evil but rather a tool for advancing God's kingdom. *Proverbs 10:4 (TLV)* declares, *"Lazy hands make for poverty, but diligent hands bring wealth."* This principle establishes that prosperity comes through dedicated effort and skillful labor. The builder recognizes that God has equipped him with talents and abilities that, when properly developed and employed, can generate resources not only for his family's provision but for the expansion of God's work on earth.

Learning skills and avoiding laziness are essential characteristics of the biblical builder. *Proverbs 6:6-8 (TLV)* instructs, *"Go to the ant,* *you sluggard! Consider her ways and be wise. Without a commander, without an overseer or ruler, she prepares her food in summer and gathers her provisions in harvest."*The ant's industrious nature serves as a model for the Messianic man who must constantly develop his abilities, pursue education, and refine his craft to increase his capacity for service and provision.

The Dichotomy of Wealth: Biblical vs. Worldly

Before we unravel this truth, we must distinguish between two opposing forces: worldly wealth and biblical wealth. Worldly wealth parades itself in gleaming excess—fleets of luxury cars, sprawling mansions, and the hollow prestige of designer labels. It is a gilded cage, mistaking accumulation for abundance. Biblical wealth, however, is forged in the fires of patience, diligence, stewardship, generosity, and legacy. It does not hoard; it multiplies—not just in gold, but in righteousness. Yet, a grave distortion plagues this conversation. Too often, *1 Timothy 6:10 (TLV)* is wielded as a weapon against prosperity itself: *"For the love of money is the root of all kinds of evil—some, longing for it, have gone astray from the faith and pierced themselves through with many sorrows."* Misquoted and misapplied, many declare, "Money is the root of all evil." But the text does not condemn currency—it condemns worship of it.

The original Greek unveils the venom beneath the surface: philargyria—a compound of philía (friendship, devotion) and árghyros (silver, money). This term, appearing only once in Scripture, is no accident. It is a warning etched in divine ink: Wealth does not corrupt—idolatry does. In fact, in the Torah, God Himself demanded a tribute to the Jewish Temple. He also demanded tithing. Money is neutral. But the lust for it? That is where the soul rots.

The Apostle Paul does not speak of coins and ledgers—he speaks of altars. Men bow before the false god of greed, trading integrity for profit, mercy for monopoly. They hoard while others hunger. They amass fortunes yet starve in spirit. Silver is lifeless—but the craving for it? That breeds deceit, exploitation, even violence. It is the delusion that wealth can replace worship, that gold can fill a void the size of God. The passage's warning is razor-sharp: Wealth is not evil—but misplaced devotion is. Greed stretches its shadow over every fortune, and those who chase it too far will wander into a darkness no riches can illuminate.

This is why biblical wealth is not merely about possession—it is about posture. A heart aligned with Heaven does not clutch its treasures; it sows them. Money is to be your servant. Not the other way around. A Messianic Man, whether he is poor or rich, will not allow an abundance of cash to sway him away from God.

Building Wealth Through Strategic Investment

The Messianic man as builder does not merely work to survive but works strategically to make his money work for him. This principle aligns with Yeshua's parable of the talents in *Matthew 25:14-30 (TLV)*, where the faithful servants multiplied their master's resources through wise investment. The builder understands that proper stewardship requires not just earning money but growing it through prudent financial decisions that honor God and serve others.

Understanding various investment vehicles becomes crucial for the builder who seeks to maximize his resources for kingdom purposes. Each financial tool serves a specific purpose in building long-term wealth and security:

Traditional IRA (Individual Retirement Account): This account allows individuals to contribute pre-tax dollars, reducing current taxable income while building retirement savings. The growth is tax-deferred until withdrawal, typically after age 59½. This vehicle helps the builder systematically prepare for his later years while reducing present tax burden.

Roth IRA: Unlike traditional IRAs, Roth contributions are made with after-tax dollars, but withdrawals in retirement are tax-free. This account is particularly valuable for younger builders who expect to be in higher tax brackets later in life, allowing tax-free growth over decades.

The Stock Market: Investment in broad market indices like the S&P 500 (represented by ETFs, or exchange trade funds, like VOO) or technology-focused funds (like QQQ) provides exposure to the growth of American enterprise. These investments allow the builder to participate in the economic expansion that benefits society while building wealth through compound growth over time. This isn't some "get-rich" tax advice. But rather a call for you to look into such things and figure how your own tactics into gaining that long-term wealth.

Health Savings Account (HSA): This triple-tax-advantaged account allows contributions, growth, and withdrawals for medical expenses to be tax-free. After age 65, it functions like a traditional IRA for non-medical expenses, making it one of the most powerful wealth-building tools available.

High-Yield Savings Account: These accounts provide higher interest rates than traditional savings while maintaining liquidity for emergency funds and short-term financial goals. They serve as the foundation of financial security, ensuring the builder can weather unexpected circumstances without compromising his long-term investments.

Real Estate Business: Property investment provides both passive income through rentals and potential appreciation over time. Real estate also serves as a hedge against inflation and offers tax advantages through depreciation deductions.

Building Homes: Construction and development businesses directly align with the builder's calling while generating substantial returns. This sector allows the Messianic man to literally build communities while creating wealth and employment opportunities for others.

Trusts: These legal entities provide asset protection, tax efficiency, and ensure wealth transfers to future generations according to the builder's values and intentions. Trusts allow the builder to maintain control over his legacy while minimizing tax burdens.

Life Insurance Policies: Whole life insurance provides both death benefits and cash value accumulation, serving as a financial foundation for the family. Term life insurance offers maximum coverage at lower cost for specific periods, protecting the family during wealth-building years.

401(k): Employer-sponsored retirement plans often include company matching, providing immediate returns on contributions. These accounts serve as the backbone of retirement planning while reducing current taxable income.

Entrepreneurial Business: An opportunity for individuals to develop a service or a product that is exchanged for income. This provides an open door for more revenue than an average W-2 job which can wisely be used to invest.

Each of these vehicles contributes to the builder's comprehensive financial strategy, allowing him to diversify risk while maximizing growth potential across different economic conditions and life stages.

The Path to Retirement and Legacy

The biblical builder views retirement not as an end to productivity but as a transition to a different form of service. His goal is not merely to accumulate wealth for personal comfort but to position himself as a blessing to future generations. ***Proverbs 13:22 (TLV)*** states, *"A good man leaves an inheritance to his children's children, but the sinner's wealth is stored up for the righteous."*

Retirement planning becomes an act of faith and stewardship, requiring the builder to make present sacrifices for future provision. This involves consistent investment in retirement accounts, real estate, and other appreciating assets that will generate income without requiring active labor. The builder approaches retirement with the understanding that his wealth should continue working for God's kingdom even when his physical capacity diminishes.

The transition from accumulation to distribution requires wisdom and careful planning. The builder must structure his assets to provide for his family's needs while supporting ministries, charitable organizations, and community development projects. This might involve establishing charitable trusts, endowments, or foundations that perpetuate his values and mission beyond his lifetime.

Legacy building extends beyond financial assets to include the transfer of wisdom, values, and spiritual inheritance to the next generation. The builder invests in educating his children about financial stewardship, business principles, and kingdom priorities. He creates systems and structures that enable his descendants to continue building God's kingdom with even greater resources and influence.

A Life-Stage Approach to Wealth Building

The Messianic man's approach to wealth building must be intentional and strategic, adapting to different life stages while maintaining consistent principles. It is never too late to begin this journey of faithful stewardship, regardless of current age or circumstances.

Ages 17-25: Foundation Building

During these formative years, the focus should be on education, skill development, and establishing good financial habits. Young men should prioritize learning marketable skills, whether through formal education, apprenticeships, or entrepreneurial ventures. Opening a Roth IRA should be a priority, even with small contributions, to take advantage of decades of compound growth. Building an emergency fund in a high-yield savings account provides financial security while learning to live below one's means. Yes, even if they are making minimum wage.

Ages 26-35: Acceleration Phase

With career establishment and potentially increased income, this period should focus on maximizing retirement contributions, particularly 401(k) accounts with employer matching. Real estate investment becomes viable, either through homeownership or rental properties. Term life insurance provides family protection during these wealth-building years. Investment in stock market index funds should increase significantly during this phase. By now, a business should be a main priority if one plans to do so.

Ages 36-45: Optimization Period

Peak earning years require sophisticated financial strategies. Maximizing contributions to all available retirement accounts, exploring real estate business opportunities, and considering whole life insurance for estate planning become priorities. Business ownership and investment in appreciating assets should accelerate wealth accumulation.

Ages 46-55: Wealth Preservation

Focus shifts to protecting accumulated wealth while continuing growth. Estate planning through trusts, comprehensive insurance coverage, and diversified investment portfolios become crucial. Consider reducing risk in investment strategies while maintaining growth potential.

Ages 56-65: Pre-Retirement Transition

Final preparations for retirement require careful planning of withdrawal strategies, healthcare costs, and legacy distribution. Maximizing catch-up contributions to retirement accounts and finalizing estate planning documents ensure smooth transition to the next phase of life.

Remember, regardless of current age, the principles of faithful stewardship apply. Those beginning later in life can still build significant wealth through diligent work, wise investment, and trust in

God's provision. The parable of the workers in the vineyard *(Matthew 20:1-16)* reminds us that God's economy operates differently than worldly systems, and faithful service is rewarded regardless of when it begins. Just remember to keep God in your finances.

Practical Budgeting for the Builder

The Messianic man must master the discipline of budgeting to ensure his resources serve God's purposes effectively. Using a monthly income of $3,000 as an example, proper stewardship requires careful allocation that prioritizes both present needs and future growth.

Housing: $1,000 (33%)
Rent or mortgage payments should not exceed one-third of gross monthly income. This provides adequate shelter while preventing housing costs from constraining other essential areas of stewardship. The builder may choose to live in a smaller space, a less expensive area, or take up a roommate to maximize resources available for investment and service.

Total Monthly Expenses: $1,500 (50%)
All living expenses including utilities, food, transportation, clothing, and miscellaneous costs should not exceed half of monthly income. This requires intentional living and careful spending decisions. The builder asks himself before each purchase: "What value does this provide?" and "Will this help me build and grow over time?"

Investment and Savings: $1,500 (50%)
The remaining $1,500 (cash you can afford to lose) should be allocated across various wealth-building vehicles:

- 401(k) contribution (especially to receive full employer match)
- Roth IRA contribution
- High-yield savings account for emergency fund
- Stock market investments through index funds
- Real estate savings for future investment
- Skills development and education

Luxury and Discretionary Spending: Minimal
The builder practices intentional frugality, recognizing that present sacrifices enable future abundance. Luxury purchases are evaluated against kingdom priorities and long-term wealth building goals.

Example of Poor Stewardship:
Consider a man who spends $1,200 on rent. His total monthly expenses equal up to $2,200 which includes rent, and $800 on luxury items and take-outs, leaving no room for investment or savings. Despite earning $3,000 monthly, he builds no wealth and remains dependent on his paycheck. This could represent the foolish builder who *"built his house on sand"* (*Matthew 7:26 TLV*).

Example of Faithful Stewardship:
A wise builder earning $3,000 monthly pays a $900 rent since he chose to room with another. He limits total expenses to $1,600, and invests $1,400 monthly across retirement accounts, stock market, and real estate savings. Even though he went slightly over half on all his monthly expenses, within ten years, his investments will generate significant passive income, enabling greater service and provision for others.

Building Up Wife, Children, and Community

The Messianic man's building extends far beyond personal wealth accumulation to encompass the development of those within his sphere of influence. His role as builder finds its highest expression in the cultivation of his family and community, understanding that true prosperity encompasses spiritual, emotional, and relational abundance.

Building Up His Wife
The builder approaches marriage as a sacred partnership where both husband and wife grow together in their service to Adonai. Following the model of Yeshua's love for the church, the husband invests in his wife's spiritual growth, emotional well-being, and personal development. This includes supporting her education, business ventures, or ministry servitude while creating an environment where she can flourish in her unique gifts and talents. If her goal is to own a bakery, the Messianic Man incorporates that goal into his itinerary and plans toward it.

Financial building with his wife involves transparent communication about goals, values, and stewardship principles. Together, they create budgets, investment strategies, and charitable giving plans that reflect their shared commitment to advancing God's kingdom. The builder recognizes that his wife's wisdom and perspective enhance their decision-making and multiply their effectiveness in both wealth building and ministry.

Building Up His Children
The builder's responsibility to his children extends beyond provision to include education in financial stewardship, work ethic, and kingdom values. We have already established in the previous chapter that from an early age, children should understand the principles of earning, saving, giving, and investing. This practical education might

include helping children start small businesses, matching their savings contributions, or involving them in family investment decisions.

More importantly, the builder instills in his children a proper understanding of wealth as a tool for service rather than an end in itself. Children learn that their privileges come with responsibilities to serve others and advance God's purposes. This foundation ensures that generational wealth becomes generational blessing rather than generational curse.

Building Up the Community Through the Church

The local congregation serves as the primary vehicle for community building, and the Messianic man actively invests in its growth and effectiveness. This involves not only financial contributions but also time, skills, and leadership. The builder might establish scholarship funds, business mentorship programs, or investment opportunities that benefit church members while strengthening the entire community.

Church investment can take many forms: funding small business loans for members, creating job opportunities within church-supported enterprises, educating members on finances and wealth-building, assisting with paying off debts, or establishing training programs that develop marketable skills. These initiatives create cycles of prosperity that benefit the entire community while demonstrating the practical relevance of biblical principles in everyday life.

The Spiritual Dimension of Building

The Messianic man recognizes that all external building must flow from internal spiritual construction. His relationship with Adonai forms the foundation upon which all other building rests, and this spiritual dimension permeates every aspect of his work and service.

Building His Relationship with God

Spiritual building requires consistent disciplines that deepen intimacy with Adonai and align the builder's heart with God's purposes. This includes regular prayer, Torah study, and meditation on Scripture. The builder approaches these practices not as religious obligations but as essential business meetings with his divine partner. Just as successful entrepreneurs maintain regular communication with their business partners, the spiritual builder maintains constant dialogue with God.

The builder also recognizes that spiritual growth occurs through challenges and testing. Financial pressures, business setbacks, and ministry obstacles serve as opportunities to develop faith, patience, and dependence on God. Rather than viewing these experiences as failures, the builder sees them as divine training that prepares him for greater responsibility and influence, both are opportunities for him to grow closer to HaShem.

Building Others Spiritually

The builder's spiritual maturity naturally overflows into the lives of others. He creates opportunities for discipleship, mentorship, and spiritual development within his family, workplace, and community. This might involve leading Bible studies, facilitating prayer groups, or simply modeling faithful living that inspires others to pursue deeper relationships with God.

Spiritual building also involves evangelism and outreach, using the builder's resources and influence to share the gospel with those who have not yet encountered Yeshua. Business relationships, community involvement, and charitable activities all become platforms for demonstrating God's love and introducing others to the transformative power of faith.

Building Kingdom Infrastructure

The builder invests in ministries, organizations, and institutions that advance God's kingdom on earth. This includes supporting local congregations, missionary work, faith-based education, and social justice initiatives that reflect biblical values. The builder approaches these investments with the same diligence and strategic thinking he applies to his business endeavors, seeking maximum kingdom impact for his contributions.

This kingdom building might involve starting ministries, funding church plants, supporting theological education, or creating media content that communicates biblical truth effectively. The builder recognizes that his wealth and influence are temporary stewardships that should be invested in eternal purposes.

Emotional Building and Leadership Development

The Messianic man's role as builder extends to the emotional and psychological development of those around him. In a world where many people are driven by emotional impulses rather than wisdom and principles, the builder provides stability, guidance, and emotional intelligence that helps others mature and thrive.

Helping Others Overcome Emotional Immaturity

The builder recognizes that many of society's problems stem from emotional immaturity—the inability to delay gratification, manage anger, overcome fear, or maintain hope in difficult circumstances. Through his example and direct intervention, he helps others develop emotional resilience and biblical responses to life's challenges.

This work requires patience, wisdom, and skill in conflict resolution, counseling, and encouragement. The builder learns to listen actively, speak truth in love, and provide practical guidance that helps others develop emotional stability. His own emotional maturity, developed through spiritual growth and life experience, becomes a resource for those struggling with anxiety, depression, anger, or other emotional challenges.

Building Up Other Men

Many men in contemporary society lack understanding of their biblical role and calling. The builder takes responsibility for mentoring other men, helping them discover their purpose, develop their gifts, and embrace their responsibilities as leaders, husbands, and fathers. This mentorship might occur through formal programs, informal relationships, or community organizations.

The builder creates environments where men can develop skills, share struggles, and support each other in their growth. This might involve business partnerships, study groups, recreational activities, or service projects that build both relationships and character. Through these efforts, the builder multiplies his impact by developing other builders who will continue the work of kingdom advancement.

Creating Emotional Security for Others

The builder's emotional stability and reliable character provide security for those in his sphere of influence. Family members, employees, and community members benefit from his consistent presence, clear communication, and trustworthy behavior. This emotional security creates conditions where others can take risks, pursue growth, and develop their own potential.

The builder also creates emotional security through his financial stability and generosity. By maintaining emergency funds, diversified investments, and multiple income streams, he positions himself to help others during financial crises. This practical assistance often opens doors for deeper ministry and relationship building.

Investing in Community Strength Through Church Financial Partnership

The Messianic man recognizes that a strong church creates a strong community, and he strategically invests in the success of church members as a form of community development. Rather than simply giving to the church, he seeks ways to create mutual benefit that strengthens both individual members and the congregation as a whole.

Creating Investment Opportunities for Church Members
The builder might establish investment funds that allow church members to participate in real estate, business ventures, or other wealth-building opportunities. These investments provide returns to participants while creating capital for larger projects that benefit the entire community. This approach teaches financial literacy while building collective wealth.

Funding Member Business Development
By providing loans, partnerships, or investment capital to church members starting businesses, the builder creates employment opportunities and economic growth within the community. These business relationships often prove more trustworthy and profitable than secular partnerships because they operate within a framework of shared values and mutual accountability.

Skills Development and Education Programs
The builder might fund training programs, educational opportunities, or certification courses that help church members develop marketable skills. These investments create human capital that benefits both individuals and the broader community while demonstrating the practical relevance of faith in everyday life.

Creating Comprehensive Community Support Systems

Through coordinated efforts with other builders in the congregation, comprehensive support systems can emerge that address various community needs. This might include credit unions, cooperative businesses, educational institutions, or healthcare initiatives that serve both church members and the broader community.

Finding and Building Godly Messianic Communities

The builder recognizes that he cannot fulfill his calling in isolation but requires partnership with like-minded believers who share his vision for advancing God's kingdom. Finding and building strong Messianic communities becomes essential for both personal growth and effective ministry.

Identifying Godly Congregations

A healthy Messianic community centers itself firmly on God's word, with leadership that demonstrates humility, integrity, and servant-heartedness. The builder seeks congregations where Torah is taught with accuracy and application, where leadership is accountable to both God and congregation, and where members are encouraged to grow in their faith and service.

Leaders in godly communities demonstrate the character described in *1 Timothy 3:1-13* and *Titus 1:5-9*, showing themselves to be humble servants of the Most High rather than authoritarian figures seeking personal gain. They invest in the spiritual and practical development of their members rather than simply collecting tithes and offerings.

Contributing to Community Building

Once connected with a godly community, the builder actively contributes to its growth and effectiveness. This involves not only financial support but also time, skills, and leadership. The builder might serve on governing boards, lead ministry initiatives, or mentor other members in their spiritual and practical development.

Messianic Men who are members of their congregation must be contributing to their community in some form. *2 Thessalonians 3:10 TLV,* *"For even when we were with you, we would give you this order: if anyone will not work, neither shall he eat."* The idea is that laziness shouldn't be tolerated in the Messianic Community. If you are a mechanic, offer to help members of your congregation, even at a decently discounted price. If you are a teacher, offer tutoring to the parents of the congregation whose child(ren) need help at a decently discounted price.

Community building also requires patience and persistence, as godly communities develop slowly through consistent faithful service rather than dramatic events or programs. The builder commits to long-term investment in relationships and systems that will benefit the community for generations.

Reproducing Healthy Communities

Mature builders eventually participate in planting new congregations or establishing satellite communities that extend the reach of biblical influence. This reproduction ensures that the principles and practices of godly community building spread to new areas and populations. If necessary, look into investing into areas that could be rebuilt for God's glory and cultivate it. It's no different from the commission Adam received from Elohim in the garden of Eden.

Always Keep In Mind. . .

Everything points to God. Whether it's your business plan, your investments, your job, etc. Everything points to God and is for the purpose of strengthening through community while fulfilling the commission to "make disciples of every nation." As a Biblicist, I strongly believe that the church is capable of assisting more in the environment God has placed them in rather than simply sit around and speak empty words all day. The purpose of your wealth is the spread the gospel through financial gains and help others grow in like manner so they can do the same. God is the focus. Where God's mystery kingdom thrives, there's no place for pride, gluttony, or greed. The goal is to see others grow spiritually, emotionally, and physically. Therefore, before anything, pray and ask God for direction.

Understanding the Spiritual Battle

The importance of being a builder in the eyes of God becomes crystal clear when we understand the spiritual opposition to this calling. Satan's strategy involves keeping men passive, dependent, and ineffective in their service to God. His voice whispers lies designed to prevent the emergence of strong, capable builders who can advance God's kingdom.

"Keep him comfortable in his mediocrity. Convince him that wealth is evil, that ambition is prideful, that building for the future is unnecessary. Let him believe that poverty is spiritual, that struggle is noble, that dependence on others is humility. Fill his mind with distractions—entertainment, instant gratification, emotional drama— anything that prevents him from developing discipline and vision. Make him reactive instead of proactive, a consumer instead of a creator, a follower instead of a leader. If he does begin to build, whisper doubts about his motives, fears about his abilities, guilt about his success. Surround him with people who will encourage his limitations rather than challenge his potential. Above all, keep him from understanding that God intends him to be a builder, a creator, a force for expansion of His kingdom. The last thing I want is a man who understands his calling to build wealth, develop others, and leave a legacy that honors the Most High." — *The Adversary*

This demonic strategy reveals why building is so crucial to God's purposes. The builder threatens Satan's kingdom by creating resources, opportunities, and influence that serve God's purposes.

Every successful business, every trained disciple, every dollar invested wisely, every skill developed represents territory taken from the kingdom of darkness and transferred to the kingdom of light.

Synopsis: The Messianic Man as Builder

The Messianic man's identity as a builder encompasses every dimension of human existence, from the spiritual to the practical, from the individual to the communal. This comprehensive calling requires him to develop himself as a complete person while simultaneously investing in the development of others and the advancement of God's kingdom.

Spiritual Building: The foundation of all building rests on the builder's relationship with Adonai. Through consistent prayer, Torah study, and obedience to God's commands, he develops the spiritual maturity necessary to handle increasing responsibility and influence. This spiritual depth enables him to discern God's will in complex situations and maintain integrity under pressure.

Financial Building: Understanding that poverty is not God's will for believers, the builder develops financial literacy and investment strategies that multiply his resources over time. Through disciplined budgeting, strategic investing, and wise stewardship, he creates wealth that serves his family, community, and God's kingdom. This financial building requires learning about various investment vehicles, maintaining emergency funds, and planning for retirement and legacy distribution.

Relational Building: The builder invests in the development of his wife, children, and community members, recognizing that true prosperity includes the flourishing of all those within his sphere of influence. This involves financial education, emotional support, spiritual mentorship, and creating opportunities for others to develop their own potential.

Emotional Building: In a world driven by emotional impulses, the builder provides stability and wisdom that helps others develop emotional maturity and biblical responses to life's challenges. His own emotional intelligence and stability become resources for those struggling with various psychological and emotional difficulties.

Community Building: Through his involvement in godly congregations and community organizations, the builder creates systems and structures that benefit multiple generations. This includes business development, educational programs, ministry funding, and infrastructure creation that serves both immediate needs and long-term community strength.

Legacy Building: The builder approaches every decision with consideration for its impact on future generations. This long-term perspective influences his investment strategies, child-rearing practices, community involvement, and ministry support. His goal is to leave behind not just financial wealth but also spiritual inheritance, practical wisdom, and institutional strength.

The Messianic man as builder recognizes that his calling extends far beyond personal success to encompass the comprehensive development of God's kingdom on earth. Through faithful stewardship of his gifts, resources, and opportunities, he participates in the divine work of creation, restoration, and redemption. His building activities serve as acts of worship, demonstrations of faith, and investments in eternity.

Every skill developed, every dollar invested, every relationship built, every person mentored contributes to the expansion of God's influence in the world. The builder understands that his temporary stewardship of earthly resources carries eternal significance, and he approaches this responsibility with the reverence, diligence, and joy that characterize those who serve the living God.

In a world that desperately needs examples of faithful masculinity, wise stewardship, and sacrificial service, the Messianic man as builder stands as a beacon of hope and a catalyst for transformation. His life demonstrates that faith and prosperity, spirituality and success, humility and influence can coexist in beautiful harmony when properly aligned with God's purposes.

The builder's ultimate goal is not personal aggrandizement but the advancement of God's kingdom and the blessing of others. Through his comprehensive approach to building—spiritual, financial, relational, emotional, and communal—he creates ripple effects that extend far beyond his immediate circumstances, touching lives, transforming communities, and advancing the purposes of Adonai for generations to come.

This is the calling of the Messianic man as builder: to be a faithful steward of God's gifts, a wise developer of His resources, a compassionate mentor to His people, and a strategic investor in His kingdom. In fulfilling this calling, he discovers that building others and serving God's purposes brings far greater satisfaction than any personal achievement, and that true success is measured not by what he accumulates but by what he contributes to the eternal purposes of the Most High.

CHAPTER EIGHT: MASTERING YOUR EMOTIONS

The Sacred Journey of Emotional Wisdom for the Messianic Man

In our contemporary society, men find themselves navigating treacherous waters when it comes to emotional expression and understanding. The modern world has created a paradox where men are simultaneously expected to be emotionally detached yet somehow intuitive leaders, stoic yet passionate, strong yet sensitive. This cultural confusion has left countless men spiritually and emotionally adrift, disconnected from the profound emotional wisdom that HaShem has woven into the very fabric of human existence.

Emotional wisdom—the divine capacity to understand, process, and express emotions in alignment with God's will—represents one of the most critical yet neglected aspects of biblical manhood. Far from being a sign of weakness, emotional mastery is a hallmark of spiritual maturity and a prerequisite for effective leadership, meaningful relationships, and authentic worship. The Messianic Man must not only develop this wisdom within himself but also learn to discern and guide the emotional landscape of others—his wife, children, community, and those under his spiritual care.

The Spiritual Architecture of Human Emotion

Before we can master our emotions, we must understand their divine purpose. Emotions are not accidents of evolution or mere chemical reactions—they are God-breathed aspects of our humanity, designed to reflect His own emotional nature. The Scriptures reveal that

HaShem Himself experiences the full spectrum of emotion: love *(1 John 4:8)*, anger *(Psalm 7:11)*, jealousy *(Exodus 34:14)*, grief *(Genesis 6:6)*, and joy *(Zephaniah 3:17)*. When we experience emotions, we are participating in an aspect of the divine image within us.

However, like all aspects of human nature, our emotions have been corrupted by sin. The fall has distorted our emotional responses, making us prone to selfishness, pride, fear, and destructive patterns. The Messianic Man must therefore approach his emotions with both reverence for their divine origin and vigilance against their corrupted tendencies.

The Five Pillars of Emotional Experience

Through careful study of Scripture and human experience, we can identify five primary emotions that form the foundation of male emotional life: love, anger, sadness, jealousy, and pride. Each of these emotions carries within it the potential for both righteousness and sin, depending on how it is understood, processed, and expressed.

The Crisis of Modern Masculinity

Contemporary society has created an emotional straightjacket for men, demanding that they suppress their God-given emotional nature in favor of an extremely hollow stoicism that masquerades as strength. This cultural deception has produced generations of men who are emotionally stunted, relationally disconnected, and spiritually immature. The consequences of this emotional illiteracy are evident everywhere: broken marriages, abandoned children, addictions, violence, and a profound sense of purposelessness that pervades masculine culture.

Men in our society have been taught to view emotions as feminine, weakness, or obstacles to success. They are encouraged to "man up," "get over it," or "push through" their feelings rather than engage with them thoughtfully and prayerfully. This approach not only contradicts biblical wisdom but also creates men who are fundamentally unprepared for the emotional demands of marriage, fatherhood, and spiritual leadership.

The tragedy is that men who cannot understand their own emotions are incapable of leading others effectively. A husband who cannot process his own anger will inevitably wound his wife and children. A father who cannot acknowledge his own sadness will be unable to comfort his children in their distress. A leader who cannot master his own pride will create division and destruction wherever he goes.

The Destructive Path: A Man Without Emotional Wisdom

Consider Dave, a 35-year-old successful businessman who embodies the modern masculine ideal. He has climbed the corporate ladder through ruthless ambition, accumulated wealth and status symbols, and maintains a carefully crafted image of success. Yet beneath this façade lies a man whose emotional immaturity has created a wake of destruction in every area of his life.

Dave's relationship with love is transactional and shallow. He views his wife as a status symbol and his children as extensions of his own ego. When his wife expresses emotional needs, he responds with irritation or dismissal, believing that his financial provision should be sufficient. He has never learned to be vulnerable, to truly listen, or to sacrifice his own desires for the good of his family. His love is conditional, selfish, and ultimately destructive.

His pride manifests as arrogance and a constant need to prove his superiority. He takes credit for every success while blaming others for failures. He cannot tolerate criticism or correction, seeing any challenge to his authority as a personal attack. His pride prevents him from genuine relationships, as he views others primarily as competition or tools for his advancement.

Dave's anger is explosive and unpredictable. When frustrated, he lashes out at subordinates, family members, or strangers with little regard for the damage he causes. He has never learned to examine the root causes of his anger or to express it constructively. His anger is self-serving, seeking to dominate rather than to protect or correct.

His jealousy is possessive and controlling. He monitors his wife's activities, sabotages colleagues who threaten his position, and harbors resentment toward anyone who appears more successful or content than himself. His jealousy stems from deep insecurity and a fundamental lack of trust in God's sovereignty over his life.

Finally, Dave's sadness is completely suppressed. He has never learned to grieve, to acknowledge loss, or to process disappointment in healthy ways. Instead, he medicates his pain with alcohol, work, or other addictions. His inability to face his own sadness has made him incapable of comforting others and has created a deep well of bitterness that poisons everything he touches.

The consequences of Dave's emotional Immaturity are predictable: his marriage is failing, his children are distant and resentful, his employees fear and dislike him, and despite his outward success, he experiences profound loneliness and emptiness. He has achieved the world's definition of masculine success while failing utterly at God's design for manhood.

The Transformative Path: A Man of Emotional Mastery

In stark contrast, consider Elijah—not the biblical prophet, but a contemporary man who has learned to walk in emotional wisdom. Elijah is a 42-year-old teacher and father of three who has devoted himself to understanding and mastering his emotions according to biblical principles.

Elijah's love is sacrificial and unconditional. He has learned to love his wife as Messiah loved the church, putting her needs above his own and seeking her spiritual and emotional well-being above his own comfort. His love for his children is patient and nurturing, combining firm boundaries with tender affection. He loves his students and colleagues not for what they can do for him but because they are image-bearers of God deserving of respect and care.

His pride is properly ordered, focusing on God's goodness rather than his own achievements. When he receives praise for his teaching or his family, he deflects credit to God and seeks to use recognition as an opportunity to glorify his Creator. He takes pride in his identity as a son of God and in the work God is doing through him, but he remains humble about his own contributions.

Elijah's anger is righteous and controlled. When he encounters injustice, sin, or threats to his family, he feels appropriate anger—but he processes it through prayer and Scripture before acting. His anger motivates him to protect the vulnerable, to confront sin lovingly, and to work for justice. He has learned to be angry without sinning, to express his anger constructively, and to seek reconciliation rather than revenge.

His jealousy is protective rather than possessive. He is jealous for his marriage covenant, his children's purity, and God's glory in his life. When he feels jealous, he examines his heart to determine whether his jealousy is righteous or selfish, and he responds accordingly. He trusts God's sovereignty over his circumstances and finds his security in his relationship with the Father rather than in comparison with others.

Elijah's sadness is acknowledged and processed biblically. When he experiences loss, disappointment, or grief, he brings these emotions to God in prayer and seeks comfort from Scripture and the Messianic Community. He has learned that sadness often deepens his dependence on God and increases his capacity for empathy and ministry to others. His willingness to be sad has made him a source of comfort and wisdom for others in their times of distress.

The fruit of Elijah's emotional maturity is evident in every area of his life: his marriage grows stronger each year, his children seek his counsel and enjoy his company, his students respect and learn from him, and his community looks to him for leadership and wisdom. He has found the secret of true masculine strength—not in emotional suppression but in emotional surrender to God's will.

The Spiritual Dimension: Finding Love in Every Emotion

The highest level of emotional wisdom comes from understanding that every emotion, when properly aligned with God's Spirit, can become a channel for divine love. This is perhaps the most profound truth about emotional mastery: the goal is not to eliminate difficult emotions but to allow the Holy Spirit to transform them into expressions of God's love.

Love as the Foundation

Love must be the lens through which we examine every emotional experience. As Scripture teaches us in 1 Corinthians 13, "love is patient, kind, not envious, not boastful, not proud, not rude, not self-seeking, not easily angered, and keeps no record of wrongs." When we filter our emotions through this definition of love, we can discern whether our emotional responses are aligned with God's will or corrupted by sin.

The Principle of Redemptive Emotional Processing: A Framework for Righteous Emotional Discipline

At the core of emotional maturity for the Messianic Man lies a singular, transformative question: "Where is the love in this?" This interrogative framework reorients emotional responses by anchoring them in divine intentionality. Anger, for instance, must be examined to determine whether it arises from a love of truth, justice, or protection of the vulnerable. Sadness ought to reflect a mourning over brokenness and a longing for restoration, while pride must be assessed for its alignment with God's glory rather than self-exaltation. Every emotion, when traced to its root, reveals an underlying impulse of love—or its distortion. Tracing the emotion to its root is understanding the reason for us feeling the way we do. By discerning this connection, the Messianic Man can evaluate whether his emotional state is righteous or sinful, ensuring his reactions align with spiritual truth.

Cognitive-Affective Vigilance: The Foundation of Emotional Mastery

To implement this principle, the Messianic Man must cultivate cognitive-affective vigilance—a disciplined awareness of his thoughts and emotions in real time. This practice is critical not only for spiritual processing but also to prevent reactive behavior that could harm himself, his family, or his community. The most challenging step is the initial recognition of an emotional surge, particularly anger. Once acknowledged, he may then engage in targeted self-inquiry:

1. "Where is the love in feeling this way?"
2. "How would Yeshua assess my actions? Is my emotional motivation pleasing to God?"

These questions facilitate immediate introspection, creating a pause between stimulus and response. Following this, the Messianic Man turns to Scripture, seeking divine wisdom to address the roots of his emotion.

From Reaction to Redemption: The Final Step

The process culminates with the question: "How can I respond to this emotion in a godly manner?" This shifts the focus from passive emotional experience to active, righteous decision-making. By

188

prioritizing rationality over impulsivity, this framework has profound practical implications: preserving marriages, preventing destructive behaviors, and even saving lives. It transforms emotions from liabilities into spiritual assets, fostering accountability and Messiah-like maturity. This concept is referred to as the Redemptive Emotional Processing (REP) Framework. This term encapsulates the core mechanism: evaluating emotions through a lens of love, aligning them with divine truth, and converting raw feelings into redemptive action.

Anger Transformed by Love

When guided by the Spirit, anger becomes a powerful force for righteousness. The Messianic Man learns to channel his anger toward sin, injustice, and threats to his family or community. His anger becomes protective rather than destructive, motivated by love for what is good rather than by wounded pride or selfishness.

This transformation requires deep self-examination and constant surrender to God's will. The man who has learned to love through his anger will find himself moved to action on behalf of the oppressed, motivated to confront sin in his own life and community, and empowered to protect those under his care. His anger becomes a tool of redemption rather than destruction.

When faced with anger, the best practical way to apply this principle is by utilizing the *REP Framework.* It will force us to examine our anger and process it biblically in order to accomplish what HaShem desires regarding any situation.

Example Scenario: Applying the REP Framework to Manage Anger and Betrayal

Consider the case of Miles, who was awaiting repayment from a friend who had repeatedly assured him that the debt would be settled the following week. However, despite receiving his own income over the past three weeks, the friend continued to delay, leaving Miles feeling disregarded and frustrated. Given the circumstances, Miles' anger is justifiable—he was given a clear promise that remained unfulfilled, leaving him feeling disrespected and exploited.

Yet, if left unchecked, this anger can fester, opening the door to sin. Resentment might manifest in destructive ways: gossip, retaliation, or even violence. Recognizing this, Miles applies the REP Framework (Recognize, Evaluate, Proceed) to process his emotions. First, he identifies the root of his anger—betrayal. His friend's broken promises eroded trust, making him feel undervalued.

Having traced his emotions to their source, Miles then reflects: Would God approve of this response? Scripture acknowledges righteous anger (Ephesians 4:26), yet it also warns against allowing bitterness to take root (Hebrews 12:15). Miles recalls how often he, too, has needed forgiveness—both from God and others. This realization leads him to Scripture, where Yeshua commands believers to forgive others as they have been forgiven (Matthew 6:14-15).

Guided by this truth, Miles chooses to release the debt, not out of obligation, but as an act of obedience and spiritual surrender. This does not mean he must loan money to this friend again; wisdom dictates setting boundaries (Proverbs 22:7). Rather, it signifies relinquishing the burden of resentment, entrusting justice and provision to Adonai. In doing so, Miles exemplifies how faith, when applied through structured reflection, can transform emotional turmoil into spiritual growth.

Sadness Transformed by Love

Sadness, when sanctified by divine love, transcends mere emotional pain and becomes a catalyst for profound spiritual maturation and compassionate ministry. The Messianic Man who has learned to grieve in alignment with Scripture discovers that his sorrow cultivates three transformative graces: empathy for others, dependence on God, and authority in comforting those who suffer (2 Corinthians 1:3-4). This redemptive shift in perspective arises from recognizing that sadness is love's rightful response to loss. In mourning the death of a loved one, we feel the anguish of love severed from its object. In lamenting personal or communal sin, we experience love's grief over the distortion of God's original design. Such sorrow is not a spiritual failure but a testament to the heart's alignment with divine values.

When submitted to the Holy Spirit, this sanctified sadness follows a sacred trajectory: it leads to healing *(Psalm 34:18)*, fuels intercession *(James 5:13)*, and deepens intimacy with God *(Matthew 5:4)*. Unlike worldly grief, which stagnates in despair, godly sorrow actively participates in restoration—bridging the gap between brokenness and redemption, both in the individual and the community.

Example Scenario: Applying the REP Framework to Manage Sorrow

James, a devoted believer, experiences deep sorrow after the sudden loss of his father. He felt that his father, a rooted believer in the Holy One of Israel and a follower of the Messiah, should not have been taken from him so early in his life. While grieving, he notices his sadness shifting between moments of quiet reflection and surges of unresolved anger. Recognizing the potential for his emotions to spiral into despair or bitterness, he intentionally applies the REP Framework to process his grief in a spiritually constructive manner.

Recognize (Identify the Emotion and Its Source)
James pauses to acknowledge his sadness rather than suppress it. Through prayer and journaling, he identifies the primary emotion: Grief over his father's absence. Next, he identifies the secondary emotion: Anger (feeling robbed of time), guilt (unresolved conversations), and fear (facing life without his father's guidance). Finally, he identifies the root cause: Love for his father, now disrupted

by death—a distortion of God's design for eternal fellowship (Revelation 21:4).

Evaluate (Assess the Emotion's Alignment with Truth)

James evaluates his feelings through a biblical lens:

- **Righteous Aspect:** His grief reflects a God-given capacity to love and value relationships *(Ecclesiastes 3:4)*.
- **Unrighteous Risk:** His anger, if unchecked, could harden into resentment toward God or others.
- **Opportunity for Growth:** This pain could deepen his reliance on God and equip him to comfort others *(2 Corinthians 1:4)*.
- **Prayerful Discernment:** "Father, show me where my grief honors You and where it needs redemption."

Proceed (Take Action Guided by the Spirit)

James intentionally channels his sorrow toward restoration:

- **Worship:** He laments through Psalms, voicing his pain while affirming God's sovereignty *(Psalm 13)*.
- **Community:** He shares vulnerably with his small group, allowing them to "mourn with those who mourn" *(Romans 12:15)*.
- **Ministry:** Later, he volunteers to mentor a young man who lost his parent, offering empathy forged in his own grief.
- **Outcome:** James's sadness, once a weight, becomes a sacred instrument—drawing him closer to God and positioning him to serve others with authenticity. Not to mention how, through daily Scripture, James comes across John 11, which gave him reassurance of His fathers resurrection. Indeed, Yeshua wept. But He used that moment as an opportunity to show the glory of God through the resurrection of

Lazarus. Indeed, Yeshua would someday resurrect his father, and that thought was sufficient to bring James peace.

Jealousy Transformed by Love

Righteous jealousy, modeled after God's own zeal for His people *(Exodus 20:5, 2 Corinthians 11:2)*, is love's protective response to threats against what is sacred. Unlike selfish jealousy—which is rooted in insecurity, control, or fear of loss—righteous jealousy arises from a commitment to uphold covenant bonds and divine truth. The Messianic Man must discern between these two motivations, ensuring his jealousy aligns with God's heart rather than human frailty.

Discerning Righteous vs. Selfish Jealousy

1. **In Marriage:**
   - Righteous: A husband's jealousy defends the exclusivity and sanctity of his marital covenant *(Malachi 2:14-16)*.
   - Selfish: Jealousy driven by insecurity or dominance stifles trust and reflects fear rather than love (*1 John 4:18*).

2. **In Parenting:**
   - **Righteous:** A father's jealousy over his children's purity seeks to guard them from corruption *(Proverbs 4:23)*.
   - **Selfish:** Jealousy that demands rigid control stems from pride, not stewardship.

Practical Example: Applying the REP Framework to Jealousy

Brad notices his wife, Sarah, frequently confiding in a male coworker. While their interactions appear innocent, Brad feels a surge of jealousy. Instead of reacting impulsively, he applies the REP Framework to discern and redeem his emotions.

1. **Recognize (Identify the Emotion and Its Source)**
   - **Emotion:** Jealousy, accompanied by anxiety and frustration.
   - **Triggers:** Sarah's emotional intimacy with another man; Brad's fear of neglect.
   - **Root Question:** Is this jealousy protective (covenantal) or possessive (insecure)?

Scriptural Lens: *"I am jealous for you with a godly jealousy" (2 Corinthians 11:2)*. David acknowledges that marriage is a covenant worthy of vigilance.

2. **Evaluate (Assess Alignment with Truth)**
   - **Righteous Aspect:** His desire to protect their marital bond reflects God's design for exclusivity **(Genesis 2:24)**.
   - **Selfish Risk:** His fear of inadequacy could distort jealousy into control or accusation.
   - **Opportunity:** To strengthen trust through communication, not coercion.

Prayerful Reflection: "Lord, purify my jealousy. Let it defend our marriage, not my ego, in Yeshua's name."

3. **Proceed (Take Redemptive Action)**
   - **Dialogue:** Brad's initiates a honest, humble conversation with Sarah: "I value our trust, but I've felt uneasy about your coworker. Can we discuss boundaries?"

- **Intercession:** He prays for their marriage rather than obsessing over threats.
- **Accountability:** He invites a mentor to help him distinguish between vigilance and insecurity.

Outcome: Brad's jealousy becomes a catalyst for deeper covenant commitment, not conflict.

Key Principles

Righteous jealousy is proactive (guarding holiness), not reactive (fueling distrust).

- **Test:** Does my jealousy lead to life (protection, prayer, trust-building) or death (control, suspicion, isolation)
- **Result:** Sanctified jealousy fuels faithfulness—in marriage, parenting, and devotion to God (James 4:5).

Pride Transformed by Love

The Paradox of Redeemed Pride

Pride, traditionally the root of humanity's fallen nature *(Proverbs 16:18)*, undergoes a radical transformation when redirected toward its divine purpose. Hence, the "R" in REP Framework The Messianic Man is called to crucify carnal pride—the exaltation of self—and instead cultivate a holy pride that celebrates God's supremacy, sonship identity *(Romans 8:16-17)*, and redemptive work through surrendered lives. This sanctified pride manifests not as arrogance but as awe, not as self-congratulation but as doxology.

The Transformation of Pride's Object

1. **From Self to Savior:**

- **Fallen Pride:** Boasting in personal achievements *(Jeremiah 9:23)*.
- **Redeemed Pride:** "Let the one who boasts boast in the Lord" *(2 Corinthians 10:17)*.

2. **From Ability to Adoption:**
   - **Fallen Pride:** Confidence in innate gifts.
   - **Redeemed Pride:** Cherishing one's position as a beloved child of God *(1 John 3:1)*.

3. **From Labor to Legacy:**
   - **Fallen Pride:** Claiming credit for outcomes.
   - **Redeemed Pride:** Celebrating God's work through yielded vessels *(John 15:5)*.

Practical Example: Applying the REP Framework to Pride

Michael, a successful entrepreneur and church leader, receives public acclaim for his nonprofit's growth. While grateful, he senses a creeping satisfaction in others' admiration. He applies the REP Framework to examine his heart.

1. **Recognize (Identify the Emotion and Its Source)**
   - **Emotion:** A warm glow of pride during applause.
   - **Triggers:** Praise for his leadership; subtle comparison to peers.
   - **Root Question:** Is this pride celebrating God's grace or my own glory?

Scriptural Lens: "What do you have that you did not receive?" *(1 Corinthians 4:7)*. "Every good gift and every perfect gift comes down from the Father" *(James 1:17)*. Michael acknowledges all gifts originate from God.

2. **Evaluate (Assess Alignment with Truth)**
   - **Holy Aspect:** Thankfulness for God's equipping *(James 1:17)*.
   - **Sinful Risk:** Claiming ownership of success *(Deuteronomy 8:17-18)*.
   - **Opportunity:** To redirect praise to God as an act of worship.
   - **Prayerful Reflection:** *"Search me, God. . .see if there is any offensive way in me"* *(Psalm 139:23-24, TLV)*.

3. **Proceed (Take Worshipful Action)**
   - **Public Declaration:** Michael shares testimonies of God's providence in meetings.
   - **Private Discipline:** He journals instances of God's intervention to combat self-reliance.
   - **Accountability:** Asks a mentor to call out any subtle arrogance.
   - **Outcome:** Michael's pride becomes a catalyst for corporate worship rather than self-promotion.

Theology of Transformed Pride

Sacred Pride is characterized by:
- **Gratitude:** "Every good gift is from above" *(James 1:17)*.
- **Humility:** "He must become greater; I must become less" *(John 3:30)*

- **Witness:** *"Let your light shine. . .that they may glorify your Father" (Matthew 5:16, TLV)*

Litmus Test: Does this pride draw attention to my own glory or God's? Does it produce thankfulness or superiority?

The Practical Path to Emotional Mastery

Understanding these principles intellectually is only the beginning. The Messianic Man must develop practical skills for emotional processing that can be applied in real-time situations. This requires disciplined practice, consistent self-examination, and dependence on the Holy Spirit's guidance.

The Practice of Emotional Awareness

The first step in emotional mastery is developing the ability to recognize and name our emotions as they arise. This requires slowing down, paying attention to our internal state, and honestly acknowledging what we are feeling. Many men have spent years suppressing their emotions so completely that they have lost the ability to identify them.

This practice begins with simple questions: "What am I feeling right now?" "Why am I feeling this way?" "What is this emotion trying to tell me?" "How should I respond to this emotion in a way that honors God?" These questions should become as natural as breathing, asked throughout the day in various situations.

The Practice of Emotional Examination

Once we can identify our emotions, we must learn to examine them biblically. This involves comparing our emotional responses to Scripture, seeking to understand the root causes of our feelings, and discerning whether our emotions are aligned with God's will or corrupted by sin.

This examination requires honesty, humility, and a willingness to be corrected by God's Word. It means acknowledging when our emotions are selfish, prideful, or destructive, and seeking transformation through repentance and surrender to the Holy Spirit.

The Practice of Emotional Expression

Finally, the Messianic Man must learn to express his emotions in healthy, constructive ways. This might mean having difficult conversations with family members, seeking counsel from wise mentors, or simply bringing our emotions to God in prayer.

Healthy emotional expression is not about venting our feelings without restraint but about communicating our emotional state in ways that build up rather than tear down, that seek understanding rather than dominance, and that invite intimacy rather than create distance.

The Ripple Effect: Emotional Leadership in the Home and Community

The man who has learned to master his emotions does not keep this wisdom to himself. He becomes an emotional leader, creating environments where others can grow in emotional maturity and spiritual health. This leadership begins in his own home and extends to his community and beyond.

Leading Through Emotional Modeling

The most powerful way to teach emotional wisdom is through modeling. When a man demonstrates healthy emotional processing, he gives permission for others to do the same. When he shows vulnerability appropriately, he creates space for authentic relationships. When he processes anger righteously, he teaches others how to channel their anger constructively.

This modeling is especially crucial for fathers, who have the opportunity to shape their children's emotional development. A father who can acknowledge his mistakes, express his feelings appropriately, and seek reconciliation when he has wronged his children teaches them invaluable lessons about emotional maturity and spiritual growth.

Creating Emotional Safety

The emotionally mature man creates environments where others feel safe to express their own emotions. He responds to others' emotional expressions with patience, wisdom, and love rather than with judgment, dismissal, or anger. This safety allows for deep relationships, authentic community, and spiritual growth.

This is particularly important in marriage, where emotional safety is essential for intimacy and trust. A husband who can receive his wife's emotions without becoming defensive, who can validate her feelings even when he doesn't understand them, and who can respond with love rather than logic creates a foundation for a thriving marriage.

Discerning Others' Emotional Needs

The mature man learns to read the emotional landscape of those around him. He can sense when his wife needs comfort, when his children need encouragement, when his colleagues need support.

This discernment comes from years of practicing emotional awareness in his own life and from seeking to understand others with the same attention he gives to understanding himself.

This skill is invaluable for leadership in any context. The man who can discern the emotional needs of his team, his congregation, or his community can provide appropriate guidance, support, and direction. He becomes a source of stability and wisdom in times of emotional turmoil.

Quick Note: Processing someone else's emotions also plays a significant role in being hidden in the Messiah. This means that everything discussed above is to be processed if one where in the opposite situation. For example, if Brad's wife (from earlier) felt jealous towards Brad's closeness with a co-worker, he is to apply the REP Framework as well. Instead of facing his wife's anger, get to the root of it. Conclusively, it is because of her love for her husband and the exclusivity of their marriage which leads to her feeling that way. Therefore, the Messianic Man responds accordingly, choosing to adjust his position for the sake of his wife. This goes for sadness, pride, etc.

The Warfare Dimension: Emotions as Spiritual Battlegrounds

The Messianic Man must understand that emotions are not neutral territory. They are active battlegrounds in the spiritual war between good and evil, between God's kingdom and Satan's kingdom. Every emotional experience presents an opportunity for either spiritual growth or spiritual decline, for the advancement of God's purposes or the advancement of the enemy's schemes.

Recognizing Spiritual Attacks

Satan and his demon legions often attack through our emotions, using them as entry points for deception, temptation, and destruction. He whispers lies in moments of anger, plants seeds of doubt in times of sadness, and inflates our pride to separate us from God and others. The emotionally mature man learns to recognize these attacks and respond with spiritual warfare rather than merely psychological techniques.

This recognition requires spiritual discernment and a deep knowledge of Scripture. When we feel overwhelmed by anger, we must ask whether this anger is righteous or whether it has been amplified by demonic influence. When we feel consumed by sadness, we must discern whether this sadness is leading us toward God or away from Him. When we feel inflated with pride, we must examine whether this pride is robbing God of glory.

Additionally, Satan has had plenty of time to study you. His demon legions are numerous and can discern your strengths from your weaknesses long before you become aware of them. They will use them to their advantage. Your weakness could be lusting. Then, the demons will tempt you with situations where you will be more inclined to lust. If your weakness is pride. Then, the demons will tempt you with circumstances that will likely make you feel prideful, whether small or great. The same goes for gluttony, greed, etc. It's our duty as the Messianic Man to overcome such temptations with vigilance and deep study of God's word.

Wielding Emotions as Spiritual Weapons

Just as Satan can use our emotions for destructive purposes, God can use our emotions as weapons in spiritual warfare. Righteous anger can motivate us to confront sin and injustice. Holy sadness can lead us to intercession and ministry. Godly jealousy can drive us to protect what is sacred and fight for what is true.

This weaponization of emotions requires submission to God's will and alignment with His purposes. Our emotions become spiritual weapons not when we use them to get what we want but when we surrender them to God's service and allow Him to channel them toward His kingdom purposes.

The Role of Scripture in Emotional Warfare

Scripture is our primary weapon in the battle for emotional maturity. When we feel overwhelmed by any emotion, we must turn to God's Word for guidance, correction, and strength. The Bible provides both diagnostic tools for understanding our emotions and therapeutic tools for healing and transformation.

This requires more than casual Bible reading. It requires memorizing the message within Scripture, meditating on the biblical truth, and allowing God's Word to reshape our emotional responses. The man who has hidden God's Word in his heart has access to spiritual resources that can transform any emotional experience into an opportunity for growth and ministry.

The Restoration Journey: Healing from Emotional Wounds

Many men come to the pursuit of emotional mastery carrying deep wounds from their past. These wounds may come from absent fathers, abusive relationships, traumatic experiences, or simply the accumulated damage of living in a fallen world. The Messianic Man must understand that emotional healing is not a luxury but a necessity for spiritual maturity and effective ministry.

Acknowledging the Wounds

The first step in healing is acknowledging that wounds exist. This requires overcoming the masculine tendency to minimize pain, to push through difficulties, and to pretend that we are unaffected by past hurts. We must have the courage to examine our emotional patterns, to identify areas of brokenness, and to seek help when needed, be it first, through God Himself. It means laying it all put before Him and trusting Him to guide you into His truth concerning your situation.

This acknowledgment is not self-pity or weakness but wisdom. Just as we would seek medical attention for a physical wound, we must seek spiritual and emotional healing for our emotional wounds. This might involve counseling, mentoring, prayer ministry, or simply honest conversation with trusted friends.

Forgiving Those Who Have Wounded Us

Forgiveness is essential for emotional healing, but it must be understood correctly. Forgiveness does not mean minimizing the harm that was done or pretending that wrong actions were acceptable. Rather, it means releasing our right to revenge and choosing to entrust justice to God.

This process often takes time and may need to be repeated multiple times. The man who has been wounded by his father may need to forgive him repeatedly as new layers of hurt are revealed. The man who has been betrayed by a friend may need to work through forgiveness as he encounters reminders of the betrayal.

Receiving God's Healing

Ultimately, emotional healing comes from God. He is the one who "heals the brokenhearted and binds up their wounds" (Psalm 147:3, TLV). The Messianic Man must learn to receive God's healing touch, to allow His love to penetrate the deepest places of hurt, and to trust His process of restoration.

This healing often comes gradually through relationship with God, through the ministry of His people, and through the application of biblical truth to our wounds. It requires patience, faith, and a willingness to be vulnerable before God and trusted others.

The Multigenerational Impact: Breaking Cycles and Building Legacy

The man who masters his emotions does not merely improve his own life; he changes the trajectory of generations. Emotional patterns, both healthy and unhealthy, are passed down from father to son, from generation to generation. The man who breaks destructive cycles and establishes healthy patterns creates a legacy that will impact his descendants for generations to come.

Breaking Destructive Patterns

Many men inherit destructive emotional patterns from their fathers and grandfathers. These might include explosive anger, emotional withdrawal, workaholism, addiction, or relational dysfunction. Destructive patterns may also include laziness, gluttony, greed, lust, etc. The Messianic Man who recognizes these patterns in his own life has the opportunity to break them and prevent their transmission to his children.

This requires honest self-examination, courageous acknowledgment of problems, and committed work toward change.

It may involve seeking professional help, joining support groups, or simply making deliberate choices to respond differently than previous generations. Ultimately, use God's word first.

Establishing Healthy Patterns

Breaking destructive patterns is only half the battle. The Messianic Man must also establish healthy emotional patterns that can be passed down to future generations. This means modeling healthy emotional expression, creating safe environments for emotional growth, and teaching emotional wisdom to his children.

This establishment of healthy patterns requires intentionality and consistency. It means having regular conversations about emotions, demonstrating healthy conflict resolution, and showing children how to process difficult feelings in godly ways. It also means developing skills such as hard work, discipline, and an eye for none other than your wife. Children will pick up on these things.

Creating a Multigenerational Vision

The emotionally mature man thinks beyond his own lifetime to consider the impact of his choices on future generations. He asks himself: "What kind of emotional legacy am I creating?" "How will my emotional patterns affect my children and grandchildren?" "What changes do I need to make to ensure that future generations are blessed rather than cursed by my emotional example?"

This vision motivates him to pursue emotional maturity not just for his own benefit but for the benefit of those who will come after him. It provides long-term motivation for the difficult work of emotional growth and creates a sense of responsibility that extends beyond his own lifetime.

Synopsis: The Integrated Life of Emotional Mastery

The journey toward emotional mastery is not a destination but a lifelong process of growth, learning, and surrender to God's will. It requires the integration of intellectual understanding, practical skills, spiritual disciplines, and relational wisdom. The Messianic Man who commits to this journey will find that it transforms not only his emotional life but every aspect of his existence.

Emotional mastery is not about becoming emotionally perfect or never experiencing difficult feelings. Rather, it is about learning to process emotions in ways that honor God, build relationships, and advance His kingdom. It is about becoming a man who can love deeply, grieve appropriately, anger righteously, and rejoice genuinely. It is about becoming a man whose emotions serve God's purposes rather than his own selfish desires.

The stakes of this journey could not be higher. The man who fails to master his emotions will inevitably wound those he loves, limit his effectiveness in ministry, and fall short of God's design for his life. The man who pursues emotional wisdom will become a source of blessing to his family, his community, and the world around him.

This is the calling of every Messianic Man: to become a man whose emotions reflect the character of God, whose emotional responses draw others toward truth and love, and whose emotional maturity creates environments where others can flourish. It is a calling that requires courage, humility, and persistent dependence on God's grace.

The path is not easy, but it is essential. The man who walks this path will discover that emotional mastery is not a burden but a blessing, not a limitation but a liberation. He will find that his emotions, when surrendered to God's will, become instruments of worship, tools of ministry, and channels of divine love.

A Prayer for the Messianic Man

Father, I come before You as Your son whom You have purchased by blood, created in Your image, called to reflect Your character in this world. Just as Yeshua prayed for His disciples, I pray for myself and for all men who desire to walk in Your ways.

Father, You have given me emotions as part of Your divine design. Help me to understand that these emotions are not accidents of biology but reflections of Your own nature. Teach me to feel what You feel, to love what You love, and to hate what You hate. May my emotions become instruments of Your glory rather than sources of my shame.

I pray that You would make me a man of God in the fullest sense—one who walks in intimate relationship with You, who seeks Your will above my own desires, and who reflects Your character in every aspect of my life. Transform my heart to be like Yours, my thoughts to align with Yours, and my emotions to serve Your purposes.

Make me a provider according to Your design—not merely one who brings home revenue, but one who provides spiritual leadership, emotional security, and godly example to my family. Help me to provide not just for their physical needs but for their spiritual growth, their emotional health, and their relationship with You. May I provide an inheritance of faith, wisdom, and righteousness that will impact generations.

Form me into a protector who guards not only against physical threats but against spiritual dangers. Give me discernment to recognize when my family is under attack—whether from external pressures, internal struggles, or spiritual opposition. Help me to create homes and communities that are sanctuaries of peace, safety, and growth. May I protect the hearts, minds, and souls of those You have entrusted to my care.

Establish me as a leader who leads by example rather than by force, who influences through love rather than through intimidation.

Help me to lead like Yeshua—with humility, sacrifice, and servant-heartedness. May my leadership draw others closer to You rather than closer to me. Give me wisdom to know when to speak and when to listen, when to act and when to wait, when to comfort and when to challenge.

If You call me to be a husband, prepare me to love my wife as Messiah loved the church. Help me to understand that marriage is not about my happiness but about Your glory. Teach me to lay down my life for my wife, to cherish her, to lead her gently, and to create an environment where she can flourish as the woman You created her to be. May our marriage be a testimony to Your love for Your people.

Should You bless me with children, make me a father who reflects Your heart. Help me to discipline with love, to teach with patience, to correct with grace, and to encourage with wisdom. May my children see You through my example and desire to follow You because of what they have experienced in our home. Give me the courage to break generational cycles of dysfunction and to establish patterns of righteousness that will bless my descendants.

Call me to be a builder—not just of physical structures but of Your kingdom. Help me to build strong families, healthy communities, and godly institutions. May everything I construct with my hands, my words, and my influence contribute to the advancement of Your purposes on earth. Give me vision to see beyond my own lifetime and to build things that will outlast me.

Above all, Father, help me to master my emotions—not by suppressing them but by surrendering them to You. When I feel anger, help me to channel it righteously. When I experience sadness, help me to grieve in ways that draw me closer to You. When I feel love, help me to express it sacrificially. When I struggle with pride, help me to boast only in You. When I face jealousy, help me to discern between selfish possession and righteous protection.

I recognize that I cannot accomplish any of these things in my own strength. Just as Yeshua depended on You for everything, I depend on You for the transformation of my heart, the renewal of my mind, and the sanctification of my emotions. Fill me with Your Spirit, guide me by Your Word, and surround me with Your people who will encourage me in this journey.

Father, I pray not only for myself but for all men who struggle with emotional immaturity, who have been wounded by their past, who feel inadequate for the tasks You have called them to. Just as You prayed for Your disciples to be one, I pray that we would be united in our pursuit of godly manhood, that we would encourage one another, hold each other accountable, and model for the world what it means to be men after Your own heart.

May our emotions become testimonies to Your goodness, our relationships become reflections of Your love, and our lives become offerings of worship to You. Help us to be the men You created us to be—not perfect, but surrendered; not without struggle, but not without hope; not without emotion, but with emotions that serve Your kingdom.

I pray these things in the name of Yeshua, who is our perfect example of manhood, our sympathetic High Priest, and our eternal King. May His life become my pattern, His love become my motivation, and His glory become my goal. In Him, I am not just a man—I am a son, a heir, and a vessel for Your purposes in this world.

Father, glorify Yourself in my life. Make me a man whose emotions reflect Your character, whose relationships demonstrate Your love, and whose legacy advances Your kingdom all throughout the ages. I surrender my emotions to You, knowing that You will transform them into instruments of Your grace and channels of Your blessing to others.

In Yeshua's name, Amen.

FINAL WORD: THE SACRED DUTY OF A MAN'S SELF IMAGE: HONOR GOD IN YOUR BODY

A man's self-image is not merely about vanity—it is a reflection of his reverence for God. The Almighty fashioned man in His image *(Gen. 1:27, TLV)*, and thus, how a man carries himself speaks volumes about his understanding of divine worth. Neglecting hygiene, dress, or physical care is not humility—it is a disregard for the temple of the Holy Spirit.

"Do you not know that your body is a temple of the Ruach ha-Kodesh who is in you, whom you have from God, and that you are not your own? For you were bought with a price. Therefore glorify God in your body." (1 Cor. 6:19-20, TLV)

A man who honors God in his appearance does so not for pride, but as an act of stewardship. The Proverbs 31 man is clothed in strength and dignity *(Prov. 31:25, TLV)*, and Yeshua Himself dressed with purpose—even His seamless tunic was of such quality that soldiers gambled for it *(John 19:23-24, TLV)*. If the King of Kings wore garments worth valuing, should we not also present ourselves with intentionality?

Why Does It Matter Spiritually?

1. **Your Body is a Witness:** When a man takes care of himself, he declares that he serves a God of order, not neglect. *"Let your light shine before men so they may see your good works and glorify your Father in heaven." (Matt. 5:16, TLV)*

2. **Respect for Others:** Sloppiness can distract from your message. Would you listen to a man who preaches discipline yet reeks of neglect? *"Do not let your adornment be external... but the hidden*

person of the heart, with the imperishable quality of a gentle and quiet spirit." (1 Pet. 3:3-4, TLV) Balance is key—neither vanity nor sloth.

3. **A Reflection of Inner Renewal:** Just as David prepared himself before the Lord *(Ps. 51:10, TLV)*, a man's outer care should mirror the inner renewal of his spirit.

A true man of God does not chase trends, but he dresses with dignity, cleanses with discipline, and carries himself with purpose—because the world should see Messiah in him before he even speaks a word.

"Let your appearance preach before your lips do."

REFLECTIONS

Take this time to reflect on the material covered in this book and the relevance it has to your own personal life. This reflective portion is centered around your growth as the Messianic Man you are called to be. Invite the Holy Spirit in as you reflect on and respond to these questions. Feel free to write your responses in the spaces below.

1) At what point in your life did you recognize that you are not living up to God's standards as a Messianic Man?

2) What are some practical ways that you can begin to walk more boldly as a Messianic Man?

3) How has your understanding of Biblical manhood changed after reading this book?

4) When you stand before God, will He recognize the man you were called to be — or will He see a stranger who traded His destiny for comfort, lust, or cowardice?

5) What secret sin are you still protecting that, if left unchecked, will rot your soul from the inside?

6) How many people have suffered—your wife, children, or brothers in faith—because you refused to lead, fight, or repent when you should have?

7) If you continue living as you are now, what kind of man will you be in 10 years? A warrior for God. . .or a hollowed-out shell of compromise? Explain.

8) Do you actually fear God—or just pretend to while living for the approval of other men?

9) How much of your "strength" is just performance—anger, ego, or control—instead of true, Messiah-like power under submission?

10) Who needed you to step up, speak truth, or intervene, but you stayed silent because it was easier?

11) If your son followed your example exactly, would he become a man of God. . .or just another casualty of this generation's weakness?

12) What mission has God given you that you've delayed or abandoned because you're afraid to lose respect, money, or safety?

13) When was the last time you truly suffered for your faith—or have you crafted a life where discipleship costs you nothing?

14) What lie do you keep telling yourself to avoid change? ("I'll repent later." "I'm not that bad." "No one will notice.")

15) If you died tonight, what would your wife, children, or Messiah say about the way you stewarded your life?

16) The Only Question That Matters: When He returns, will He find faith in you—or will you be just another man who knew the truth. . .but didn't live it?

17) Are you aware that God watches you at all times?

18) "For man looks at the outward appearance, but Adonai looks into the heart." (1 Samuel 16:7, TLV)

Does your strength come from the Spirit—or from rage, posturing, or the fear of other men?

19) "For everything in the world—the desire of the flesh, the desire of the eyes, and the pride of life—is not from the Father." (1 John 2:16, TLV)

Which of these three graves are you digging for yourself?

20) "But if anyone does not provide for his own, especially his household members, he has denied the faith and is worse than an unbeliever." (1 Timothy 5:8, TLV)

In what way have you starved those you were meant to nourish—spiritually, emotionally, or physically?

21) "If anyone wants to come after Me, let him deny himself, take up his cross, and follow Me." (Matthew 16:24, TLV)

What cross have you laid down because the weight was too costly?

22) "Today, if you hear His voice, do not harden your hearts."
    (Hebrews 3:15, TLV)

What is the Spirit saying to you right now that you're still bargaining against?

23) "Why do you call Me, 'Lord, Lord,' and not do what I say?"
    (Luke 6:46, TLV)

Is your worship just noise—unbacked by obedience?

24) Which verse in this book pierced you deepest? Why?

25) What truth here do you most want to ignore? (That is likely where your battle lies.)

26) If you lived out one chapter with total faithfulness, how would your legacy change?

27) Who in your life needs these words? Will you give them—or withhold life to avoid discomfort?

28) Will this book be a turning point for you. . .or just another marker on the road of delay?

FINAL CHARGE:

"Choose for yourselves this day whom you will serve. . .But as for me and my household, we will serve Adonai." (Joshua 24:15, TLV)

The choice is yours. What will it be? Who will you choose? Whom will you serve?

AUTHOR INFO

Joel Maxwell was born and raised in Jamaica under the Roman Catholic way of worship before discovering the depth through conversion to the Orthodox Jewish faith after migrating to America, learning how to properly dissect the Tanakh. However, he still felt something missing behind all of the ritualistic devotions and sought to find the correlation between Christianity and Judaism, asking himself, "Where does Yeshua fit into all of this?" After God led him to the Messianic Community in Florida, he chose to take up tutelage from several Rabbi's who were once themselves Jews who came to faith in Yeshua. Now, he takes up the mantle and devoted himself to sharing God's truth to those whom God has appointed for him in humility. That truth is: God, through Yeshua, died for our sins and resurrected.